UNITED NATIONS CONFERENCE ON TRADE AND DEVELOPMENT

D1563237

FAIR AND EQUITABLE TREATMENT

UNCTAD Series on Issues in International Investment Agreements II

UNITED NATIONS
New York and Geneva, 2012

NOTE

As the focal point in the United Nations system for investment and technology, and building on 30 years of experience in these areas, UNCTAD, through the Division on Investment and Enterprise (DIAE), promotes understanding of key issues, particularly matters related to foreign direct investment (FDI). DIAE assists developing countries in attracting and benefiting from FDI by building their productive capacities, enhancing their international competitiveness and raising awareness about the relationship between investment and sustainable development. The emphasis is on an integrated policy approach to investment and enterprise development.

The term "country" as used in this study also refers, as appropriate, to territories or areas. The designations employed and the presentation of the material do not imply the expression of any opinion whatsoever on the part of the United Nations Secretariat concerning the legal status of any country, territory, city or area or of its authorities, or concerning the delimitation of its frontiers or boundaries. In addition, the designations of country groups are intended solely for statistical or analytical convenience and do not necessarily express a judgment about the stage of development reached by a particular country or area in the development process.

The following symbols have been used in the tables:

Two dots (..) indicate that data are not available or are not separately reported.

Rows in tables have been omitted in those cases where no data are available for any of the elements in the row.

A dash (–) indicates that the item is equal to zero or its value is negligible.

A blank in a table indicates that the item is not applicable.

NO LOANS
UN2
TD/UNCTAD/DIAE/IA/2011/5

A slash (/) between dates representing years, e.g. 1994/1995, indicates a financial year.

Use of a dash (–) between dates representing years, e.g. 1994–1995, signifies the full period involved, including the beginning and end years.

Reference to "dollars" ($) means United States dollars, unless otherwise indicated.

Annual rates of growth or change, unless otherwise stated, refer to annual compound rates.

Details and percentages in tables do not necessarily add to totals because of rounding.

The material contained in this study may be freely quoted with appropriate acknowledgement.

UNCTAD/DIAE/IA/2011/5

UNITED NATIONS PUBLICATION
Sales No. E.11.II.D.15
ISBN 978-92-1-112827-7

PREFACE

This volume is part of a series of revised editions – sequels – to the UNCTAD Series on Issues in International Investment Agreements. The first generation of this series, also called the Pink Series, was published between 1999 and 2005 as part of UNCTAD's work programme on international investment agreements (IIAs). It aimed at assisting developing countries in participating as effectively as possible in international investment rule making at the bilateral, regional, plurilateral and multilateral levels. The series sought to provide balanced analyses of issues that may arise in discussions about IIAs and has since then become a standard reference tool for IIA negotiators, policymakers, the private sector, academia and other stakeholders.

Since the publication of the first generation of the Pink Series, the world of IIAs has changed tremendously. In terms of numbers, the IIAs' universe has grown, and continues to do so – albeit to a lesser degree. Also, the impact of IIAs has evolved. Many investor-State dispute settlement (ISDS) cases have brought to light unanticipated – and partially undesired – side effects of IIAs. With its expansive – and sometimes contradictory – interpretations, the arbitral interpretation process has created a new learning environment for countries and, in particular, for IIA negotiators. Issues of transparency, predictability and policy space have come to the forefront of the debate – so has the objective of ensuring coherence between IIAs and other areas of public policy, including policies to address global challenges, such as the protection of the environment (climate change) or public health and safety. Finally, the underlying dynamics of IIA rule making have changed. A rise in South–South FDI flows and emerging economies' growing role as outward investors – also with respect to the developed world – are beginning to alter the context and background against which IIAs are being negotiated.

It is the purpose of the sequels to consider how the issues described in the first-generation Pink Series have evolved, particularly focusing on treaty practice and the process of arbitral interpretation. Each of the sequels will have similar key elements, including (a) an introduction explaining the issue in today's broader context; (b) a stocktaking of IIA practice and arbitral awards; and (c) a section on policy options for IIA negotiators, offering language for possible new clauses that better take into account the development needs of host countries and enhance the stability and predictability of the legal system.

The updates are conceptualized as sequels, that is to say, they aim to complement rather than replace the first-generation Pink Series. Compared with the first generation, the sequels will offer a greater level of detail and move beyond a merely informative role. In line with the mandate entrusted to UNCTAD, they will aim to analyse the development impact and strengthen the development dimension of IIAs. The sequels are finalized through a rigorous process of peer reviews, which benefit from collective learning and sharing of experiences. Attention is placed on ensuring the involvement of a broad set of stakeholders, aiming to capture ideas and concerns from society at large.

The sequels are edited by Anna Joubin-Bret, and produced by a team under the direction of Jörg Weber and the overall guidance of James Zhan. The members of the team include Bekele Amare, Hamed El-Kady, Jan Knörich, Sergey Ripinsky, Diana Rosert, Claudia Salgado, Ileana Tejada and Elisabeth Tuerk.

This paper is based on a study prepared by Peter Muchlinski and Sergey Ripinsky. Claudia Salgado, Elisabeth Tuerk and Hamed El-Kady provided inputs. The UNCTAD secretariat gratefully acknowledges the comments on the draft version of this paper, received from Stanimir Alexandrov, Andrea Bjorklund, James Crawford, Roberto Echandi, Joern Griebel, Chen Huiping, Andrea Saldarriaga, Stephan Schill, Brigitte Stern and Christopher Thomas.

The paper does not represent the views of any of the aforementioned peer reviewers. The research was facilitated by the access to the beta version of the Investor-State Law Guide, or ISLG, database. The paper also benefited from an online discussion on UNCTAD's network of IIA experts on the issue of fair and equitable treatment.

Supachai Panitchpakdi
Secretary-General of UNCTAD

February 2012

CONTENTS

BOXES

ABBREVIATIONS

ASEAN	Association of Southeast Asian Nations
BIT	bilateral investment treaty
CIL	customary international law
COMESA	Common Market for Eastern and Southern Africa
EFTA	European Free Trade Association
EPA	economic partnership agreement
FDI	foreign direct investment
FET	fair and equitable treatment
FTA	free trade agreement
FTC	Free Trade Commission
GATT	General Agreement on Tariffs and Trade
GATS	General Agreement on Trade in Services
ICJ	International Court of Justice
ICSID	International Centre for Settlement of Investment Disputes
IIA	international investment agreement
ISDS	investor-State dispute settlement
MFN	most-favoured-nation treatment
MST	minimum standard of treatment of aliens under customary international law
NAFTA	North American Free Trade Agreement
OECD	Organisation for Economic Cooperation and Development
UNCITRAL	United Nations Commission on International Trade Law
WTO	World Trade Organization

EXECUTIVE SUMMARY

The obligation to accord fair and equitable treatment (FET) to foreign investments appears in the great majority of international investment agreements (IIAs). Among the IIA protection elements, the FET standard has gained particular prominence, as it has been regularly invoked by claimants in investor-State dispute settlement (ISDS) proceedings, with a considerable rate of success.

The wide application of the FET obligation has revealed its protective value for foreign investors but has also exposed a number of uncertainties and risks. First, with regard to the capacious wording of most FET provisions, many tribunals have interpreted them broadly to include a variety of specific requirements including a State's obligation to act consistently, transparently, reasonably, without ambiguity, arbitrariness or discrimination, in an even-handed manner, to ensure due process in decision-making and respect investors' legitimate expectations. This extensive list of disciplines can be taxing on any State, but especially developing and least-developed ones. The second issue concerns the appropriate threshold of liability, that is, how grave or manifest a State's conduct must be to become FET-inconsistent. Thirdly, the application of FET provisions has brought to light the need to balance investment protection with competing policy objectives of the host State, and in particular, with its right to regulate in the public interest.

As far as treaty practice is concerned, IIAs employ the following main formulations and approaches of the FET standard:

(a) Unqualified obligation to accord fair and equitable treatment;

(b) FET obligation linked to international law;

(c) FET obligation linked to the minimum standard of treatment of aliens under customary international law;

(d) FET obligation with additional substantive content such as denial of justice.

The actual practice of application of FET clauses by arbitral tribunals has drawn a distinction solely between FET as an unqualified standard and the FET obligation linked to the minimum standard of treatment of aliens under customary international law.

Historically, the FET standard – regardless of how it is expressed – came into existence as an expression of the minimum standard of treatment. However, where the FET obligation is not expressly linked textually to the minimum standard of treatment of aliens, many tribunals have interpreted it as an autonomous, or self-standing one. Instead of deriving the content of the standard from its original source (customary international law), these tribunals chose to focus on the literal meaning of the provision itself.

The question of the relationship between FET and the minimum standard of treatment of aliens has received particular attention in the ISDS cases brought under the North American Free Trade Agreement (NAFTA), where the two standards are expressly linked. Although not all NAFTA decisions have interpreted the FET obligation consistently, the view has been gaining dominance that for a breach to be found, a State's conduct must be "egregious" or "shocking" from an international perspective (high liability threshold) and that, for example, a simple illegality under domestic law is not sufficient to establish a violation of the minimum standard of treatment. Importantly, however, the understanding of what can be seen as egregious has evolved since the 1920s, when this test had been conceptualized.

NAFTA cases have also exposed certain problems of applying FET as part of the minimum standard of treatment of aliens, in particular that the latter was largely developed in the context of claims regarding treatment of individuals (not businesses), outside the context of economic policymaking. Furthermore, given that the minimum standard of treatment of aliens forms part of customary international law, a claimant would carry a heavy burden of demonstrating general and consistent State practice and *opinio juris* in order to show that the minimum standard incorporates a certain substantive requirement. For these reasons, a link between FET and the minimum standard of treatment has been mostly useful, not from the point of view of the substantive content of the obligation, but as an expression of the gravity of the conduct required for that conduct to be held in violation of the standard.

Tribunals established under IIAs other than NAFTA and applying FET clauses not linked to the minimum standard of treatment of aliens have on the whole been paying less attention to the discussion of the applicable liability threshold. Some of them have suggested that it is "a high one"; others held the view that it is lower than under the minimum standard of treatment, while most did not address the matter. At the same time, non-NAFTA tribunals have tended to allow some inefficiency, trial and error, and imperfection in a government's conduct and have accepted that a violation by the host State of an investment contract or of its own domestic law does not necessarily amount to a breach of the FET standard.

The substantive content of the FET standard (specific requirements comprising it) has been fleshed out by arbitral tribunals on a case-by-case basis. It is a continuing development, which is reinforced by the practice of tribunals to refer to, and discuss, earlier awards. Although each tribunal interprets a FET provision from the investment treaty applicable in that specific case, there has been considerable convergence in terms of the elements that the FET standard incorporates, regardless of how it is expressed in the treaty. The following five main concepts have emerged as relevant in the context of fair and equitable treatment:

(a) Prohibition of manifest arbitrariness in decision-making, that is, measures taken purely on the basis of prejudice or bias without a legitimate purpose or rational explanation;

(b) Prohibition of the denial of justice and disregard of the fundamental principles of due process;

(c) Prohibition of targeted discrimination on manifestly wrongful grounds, such as gender, race or religious belief;

(d) Prohibition of abusive treatment of investors, including coercion, duress and harassment;

(e) Protection of the legitimate expectations of investors arising from a government's specific representations or investment-inducing measures, although balanced with the host State's right to regulate in the public interest.

In this regard, the investor's own conduct has also featured as a relevant factor in assessing FET claims. Specifically, fraud or misrepresentation on an investor's part can justify governmental interference. The investor is also under the obligation to perform full due diligence in order to independently assess the risks involved in making an investment in a particular State, as well as to manage its investment in a sound manner.

The question of measuring compensation for breaches of the FET obligation has not yet received much attention from arbitral tribunals. It appears, however, that the compensation stage potentially allows additional room for balancing of relevant interests. It may be useful to allow tribunals the flexibility to adjust the amount of compensation in light of the circumstances of the case and equitable considerations, in particular to award less than full compensation where the measure at issue, while eventually breaching the FET standard, is at least partially explained by legitimate considerations or there are other mitigating circumstances, such as the claimant's own conduct.

The last section of the paper discusses the policy options available to negotiators. They include omission of the FET clause from treaties, expressing it with or without reference to sources and qualifications as well as replacing the general obligation to grant fair and equitable treatment with more specific requirements and further clarifications designed to provide more certainty and predictability. Additional policy options concern the IIA preambles, which often influence the interpretation of the FET provision, as well as explicit language to ensure the State's unrestricted prerogative to regulate in the public interest. All of these options can be explored in new IIA negotiations, as well as when guiding the interpretation of existing treaties.

INTRODUCTION

The fair and equitable treatment (FET) standard is a key element in contemporary international investment agreements (IIAs). Over the years, it has emerged as the most relied upon and successful basis for IIA claims by investors.

The standard protects investors against serious instances of arbitrary, discriminatory or abusive conduct by host States. As such, it constitutes an important investment protection element of IIAs. At the same time, the vague and broad wording of the obligation carries a risk of an overreach in its application. The central concern of the present paper is that the FET standard may be applied in investor-State arbitration to restrict host-country administrative and governmental action to a degree that threatens the policymaking autonomy of that country. This arises out of the uncertainty regarding the correct approach to interpretation and application of the standard. On the one hand, there is the issue of which sources of law should be used when determining the proper limits of the discretion to interpret the standard. On the other, there is the question of the actual substantive content of the standard.

This issue is complicated by the existence of differing formulations of the FET standard in IIAs. Some use an unqualified FET provision that simply states that investments shall be accorded fair and equitable treatment, while others qualify this statement with references to the source of the obligation, be it international law, customary international law or the minimum standard of treatment of aliens under customary international law. The precise impact of such wording has been controversial. Indeed, some tribunals have disregarded the sources of the FET standard and concentrated purely on the content of the standard based on case-by-case readings of what is fair or equitable in light of the specific facts. This has been the case particularly when tribunals have been applying an unqualified FET clause, which lends itself to a more general fairness and equity appraisal.

In other cases, tribunals have struggled with the source of the obligation, particularly with the minimum standard of treatment of aliens under customary international law, when seeking to establish the actual meaning of the standard.

As interpreted by arbitral tribunals, the FET standard raises highly complex and contentious issues as to the types of administrative and governmental action that can be reviewed under the standard and the degree of seriousness of breach that is required to activate a compensable claim. In relation to the latter, there has been a noticeable trend in arbitral practice away from the classic customary international law standard of treatment of aliens towards a less stringent reading of the standard.

This approach, taken by a number of tribunals, increases the chances that a wide range of State regulations or measures can be found to infringe the FET standard including those that have a legitimate public purpose. Therefore, this approach poses special challenges for developing countries where the State may be required to intervene in the economy and introduce legislative or regulatory changes more frequently or of a greater magnitude.

Of course, any State intervention must observe basic standards of good governance, but an expansive approach to the interpretation of the FET standard, including through overreliance on the doctrine of investors' legitimate expectations, poses a risk leading to the creation of unbalanced results in the determination of what is contrary to good governance. In particular, an expansive interpretation of minimalist treaty language can give rise to a lack of predictability in the application of the standard. This, in turn, may lead to the undermining of legitimate State intervention for economic, social, environmental and other developmental ends.

The vagueness of the FET standard is at the core of the problem. As will be seen in section II, IIAs often contain a general statement to the effect that the parties will accord fair and equitable treatment to the investments of investors from the other contracting party. There is no attempt to define what this means. As Schill explains:

> *"Fair and equitable treatment does not have a consolidated and conventional core meaning as such nor is there a definition of the standard that can be applied easily. So far it is only settled that fair and equitable treatment constitutes a standard that is independent from national legal order and is not limited to restricting bad faith conduct of host States. Apart from this very minimal concept, however, its exact normative content is contested, hardly substantiated by State practice, and impossible to narrow down by traditional means of interpretative syllogism."* (Schill, 2009, p. 263).

The challenge posed to negotiators in this environment of uncertainty is to establish clearer boundaries as to the types of conduct that constitute a violation of the FET obligation or, conversely, those that may not be considered as breaching the IIA in question. In doing so, a right balance needs to be struck between investment protection, on the one hand, and the preservation of the freedom of legitimate State action, on the other. This lies at the heart of the development *problématique* of the FET standard.

This sequel to the Fair and Equitable Treatment IIA Issues Paper seeks to review existing treaty practice, identify the impact of arbitral interpretation and offer options for IIA negotiators, particularly as far as the development dimension of these options is concerned. Section I looks at the historical origins of the FET standard and identifies the key issues raised by the standard and its application in practice. Section II examines the main approaches for defining FET in IIAs. Section III focuses on the interpretation of the standard by arbitral tribunals in investor-State disputes. It first looks at the controversial question of the relationship between the FET standard and the international minimum standard of treatment of aliens and then goes on to consider the specific elements of content of the FET standard that have emerged from arbitral practice to date.

Finally, section IV provides a list of policy options and formulations for negotiators, including those aimed at making the application of the standard more predictable and conducive to the right of States to regulate in the public interest.

I. EXPLANATION OF THE ISSUE

A. Key characteristics of the standard

1. Historical origins

Standards of treatment based on fairness and equity pre-date modern IIAs. FET clauses used in BITs and other IIAs appeared in early international economic agreements such as the Havana Charter for an International Trade Organization (1948) and the Economic Agreement of Bogotá (1948), as well as in the United States Friendship, Commerce and Navigation (FCN) treaties. The first use of the FET clause in the IIA context can be traced back to Article I of the Draft Convention on Investments Abroad proposed by Hermann Abs and Lord Shawcross in 1959:

> *"Each Party shall at all times ensure fair and equitable treatment to the property of the nationals of the other Parties. Such property shall be accorded the most constant protection and security within the territories of the other Parties and the management, use and enjoyment thereof shall not in any way be impaired by unreasonable or discriminatory measures"* (Abs and Shawcross, 1960)

This initiative was followed by the Organisation for Economic Cooperation and Development (OECD), which produced its own Draft Convention on the Protection of Foreign Property, known as the Draft OECD Convention, which included a fair and equitable treatment clause along similar lines. In its notes and comments to Article 1, a clear reference was made to the source of the standard: "the standard required conforms to the 'minimum standard' which forms part of customary international law" (OECD, 1967, p. 120). It is important to note here that the Draft OECD Convention was used by most OECD countries as the basis for their IIA negotiations. By referring to the OECD model and using it systematically, they are also referring to this standard as defined by the Draft Convention of 1967.

As will be further discussed below, the reference to fair and equitable treatment in IIAs has created a controversy about whether the FET standard is *autonomous*, that is, has a content of its own, or whether it is limited to the minimum standard of treatment of aliens under customary international law. In the words of one author, "[i]f the historical background is to be taken seriously, then the FET standard when first used, could not have meant anything higher than the [international minimum standard of treatment]" (Montt, 2009, p. 69). However, many arbitral tribunals have decided otherwise and gave the FET standard a life and a source of its own.

The contemporary meaning of the FET standard rests on interpretations by individual ad hoc arbitral tribunals with no effective appellate review. This opens the standard to inconsistent interpretations resulting in the uncertainty regarding its meaning, since treaties do not define its content, but typically refer, as noted above, to an unqualified formulation of the standard, or to one qualified by references to (customary) international law. As far as the customary international minimum standard of treatment is concerned, uncertainty is compounded by the lack of uniform acceptance of State practice in this area.

2. Definition, sources and content of the standard

(i) Definition of terms

The fair and equitable treatment standard is an absolute standard of protection. It applies to investments in a given situation without reference to how other investments or entities are treated by the host State. Thus host governments are unable to resist a claim under this standard by saying that the treatment is no different from that experienced by their own nationals or other foreign investors operating in their economy.

In relation to usage in BITs, the original purpose and intent behind FET clauses was to protect against the many types of situations of how unfairness may manifest itself, such as, for example, an arbitrary cancellation of licences, harassment of an investor through unjustified fines and penalties or creating other hurdles with a view to disrupting a business. Here the standard would provide a gap-filling device, as not all kinds of unfair administrative or governmental conduct could be subsumed under the more specific non-discrimination or protection-of-property standards contained in BITs (Dolzer and Schreuer, 2008, p. 122).

Until the recent rise of arbitral interpretations of the FET standard, its meaning was not generally determined. The word "fair" is defined by the *Concise Oxford Dictionary* as "just, unbiased, equitable, in accordance with rules".[1] Therefore, fairness connotes, among other things, equity. The concepts of fair and equitable are, to a large extent, interchangeable. In addition, equity suggests a balancing process, weighing up of what is right in all the circumstances. It is a word related to the idea of equilibrium defined as "a state of physical balance".[2] The balancing function of equity is accepted as an aspect of international law.[3] Thus, based on a plain meaning of the words, "fair and equitable" treatment requires an attitude to governance based on an unbiased set of rules that should be applied with a view to doing justice to all interested parties that may be affected by a State's decision in question, including the host State's population at large.

(ii) Sources of the standard

As alluded to above, a further problem that manifests itself in the interpretation of the FET standard is the extent to which it can be seen as having its source in international law or, more specifically, in customary international law. There has been much debate on whether the FET standard should be interpreted in the light of the international minimum standard of treatment of aliens, or whether it is a self-standing standard. To a large extent, this discussion stems from the fact that the language of the relevant IIAs differs significantly. Some agreements expressly link the FET standard to international law, or to the minimum standard of treatment of aliens under customary international law, while others refer only to fair and equitable treatment without any further qualification. It should be reiterated, however, that the origins of the FET obligation – whether qualified or unqualified – are found in the Draft OECD Convention that links the FET standard to customary international law.

Further, as will be shown in section III, arbitral awards are not uniform in this regard – even with respect to FET clauses of the same type. At the same time, identification of the correct source of the FET standard – whether it is grounded in customary international law or is a self-standing obligation – can have important consequences in terms of the standard's content and, more precisely, of the types of State measures that can be challenged as well as the required threshold for finding a violation, that is, the required degree of seriousness of the breach.

There are some considerations that, with time, can lead to the convergence of the international minimum standard and the unqualified FET standard as far as the actual content of the obligation is concerned. Firstly, some elements of the two standards clearly overlap, such as the requirement of due process or denial of justice. Secondly, it has been argued that the minimum standard of treatment of aliens is not fixed in time and that its content can evolve. Therefore, it would be worthwhile to examine how minimum standard of treatment has developed over time.

(iii) Content of the standard

The sources for determining the content of the international minimum standard rely to a large extent on the pronouncements of mixed claims commissions that have considered the treatment of natural persons. Accordingly, the standard set out therein would emphasize issues of denial of justice or extreme abuse of persons in custody (Paparinskis, 2009). Property claims were much rarer and occurred mainly in connection with "damage that took place during social upheavals and revolutionary situations that posed a danger to life and to property" (Sornarajah, 2010, p. 130; McLachlan et al., 2007, p. 216). The relationship between the denial of personal justice and denial of property rights was thus not entirely clear in early arbitral decisions. It was only in the early to mid-twentieth century that norms relating to expropriation became more settled, and even these were subject to an intense conflict between the capital-exporting countries of the West and developing capital-importing countries, and countries following a socialist economic model for much of that century Accordingly, the legal building blocks for the analysis of the international minimum standard and its role in international investment law are precarious and often incomplete, vague and contested (see Salacuse, 2010, pp. 75–76). As a result, the role to be played, in particular by the tribunals working before the BIT era, has been a source of considerable debate.

A critical issue of interpretation arises out of the increased reference by arbitral tribunals to the notion of investors' legitimate expectations. This concept is not referred to in actual FET provisions. As such, it is an arbitral innovation. When economic, regulatory or other conditions general or specific to the investment undergo changes negatively affecting the investment's value, they may be seen as a breach of legitimate expectations prevailing at the time the investment is made. While in principle the concept of legitimate expectations may well have a place within fair and equitable treatment, its thoughtless application, looking at the issues at hand from the perspective of the investor only, runs the risk that the true purpose of the FET provision in IIAs will be lost under the weight of investor concerns alone. In this context, it is crucial to understand what kind of investor expectations can be seen as legitimate and in what circumstances they may reasonably arise. Further, it is necessary to strike a balance between the expectations of the investor and those of the host country and host community in order to establish approaches to interpretation reflecting the actual social and policy context in which foreign investors find themselves. In this regard, investor conduct and the expectations of the local community as a result of the investment will be relevant considerations stemming from the nature of the standard.

Further elements forming the content of the FET obligation are discussed in section III.B.

B. Key development issues

In addition to being the most frequent basis for ISDS claims, the FET norm has the potential to reach further in the traditional *domaine réservé* than any other IIA provision (Dolzer, 2005, p. 964). One commentator noted that "[i]t is both fascinating and astonishing that fair and equitable treatment has developed from an almost vacant expression into an obligation of such potential breadth within a few years" (Kläger, 2010, p. 443). Historically, the expropriation standard has been more important; however, mass nationalizations have become increasingly rare and have given way to less intrusive tools of host countries' economic policy measures. This, as well as the open-ended nature of the FET standard, has turned FET claims into a popular litigation strategy. Nowadays, in addition to other heads of claim, practically each case features an allegation of the respondent's breach of the FET standard.

The popularity of a FET claim increases the challenges faced by IIA stakeholders and emphasizes a number of key development and sovereignty-related issues:

(a) An expansive interpretation of the FET standard and a lack of predictability as to what kinds of actions will infringe upon it;

(b) The indeterminacy of the threshold of liability under the FET standard;

(c) The potential for striking an inadequate balance between the private and public interests affected by the administrative or governmental decision under scrutiny.

1. Expansive interpretation and lack of predictability

As discussed in section III, many arbitral awards have interpreted the FET concept rather broadly, especially in cases relying on the legitimate expectations of the investor. The result may be an open-ended and unbalanced approach, which unduly favours investor interests and overrides legitimate regulation in the public interest. In addition, although different types of language used in treaties may require different interpretation, in practice tribunals tend to justify their findings by reference to earlier awards. A kind of de facto doctrine of precedent evolves that can tempt a tribunal to find an infringement because an infringement was earlier found in an apparently similar case of maladministration. At the same time, as there is no official doctrine of precedent in international law, it is uncertain whether an earlier award will be followed or not, thereby increasing the lack of predictability in the decision-making process.

As mentioned earlier, the wording of most FET clauses is minimalist. Such language, lacking specific meaning, is particularly prone to expansive interpretation simply because an arbitral tribunal does not have sufficient interpretative guidance from the treaty. In particular, the emphasis on investor protection placed by the preambles in many IIAs may as the main objective of the treaty lead a tribunal to adopt a reading of the FET clause against this background (pro-investor).

The lack of predictability is further increased by the absence of a clear legal test of fair and equitable treatment. Ultimately, the decision may rest on little more than whether, in the circumstances of the specific case, the tribunal feels that the investor had been treated fairly or not. It has even been suggested that due to its extreme vagueness the FET obligation lacks legitimacy as a legal norm.[4]

In a system without binding precedent, involving different and independent ad hoc tribunals applying the vaguely worded standard to different facts and under different treaties, it is difficult to expect consensus and consistency in understanding the FET standard and its specific elements.

These divergent approaches based on capacious wording may result in a real challenge for States to implement the FET obligation domestically. This is even more challenging when State agencies or subnational entities are the ones interacting with the investor or in charge of taking a regulatory measure or implementing it. If the State and its subnational entities do not know in advance what type of conduct may be considered a breach of a treaty, then it cannot organize its regulatory and administrative decision-making processes and delegation in a way that ensures that its conduct will not incur liability under the FET standard. This may in turn generate unwarranted effects such as possible regulatory chill or positive discrimination in favour of foreign investors against domestic investors.

2. Setting the liability threshold

As far as the scope of the FET is concerned, current arbitral practice shows that all types of governmental conduct – legislative, administrative and judicial alike – can potentially be found to breach the FET obligation. In terms of the standard's content, there are two relevant aspects: (a) the principles of good governance, against which the conduct will be assessed (due process, absence of arbitrariness in decision-making, non-frustration of legitimate expectations and so forth) and (b) the threshold of liability, that is, how serious the breach must be in order for a violation to be found. While both of these aspects can be influenced by the ultimate source of the FET obligation – whether autonomous or grounded in international law – the source is particularly relevant to determine the liability threshold.

Thus, where an IIA ties the FET obligation to the customary international law minimum standard of treatment of aliens, the threshold of liability as applied by arbitral tribunals has been generally higher: the State's conduct needs to be egregious or outrageous in accordance with the *Neer* case. Indeed, the minimum standard of treatment of aliens is the *minimum* standard, an international lowest common denominator or a floor for the assessment of governmental conduct. The understanding of what is viewed as egregious conduct may well have evolved since the 1920s;[5] also, a determination of what is egregious, manifest or flagrant involves a degree of subjectivity. Nonetheless, a reference in an FET clause to the minimum standard of treatment of aliens conveys a clear message that only the very serious acts of maladministration can be seen as violating the treaty.

In contrast, arbitral tribunals applying unqualified FET clauses have not limited themselves to the most serious breaches and have found violations of the FET standard where they considered the State's conduct in question to be simply unfair towards the claimant.

Even though many tribunals, including those applying the unqualified FET clauses, tend not to find violations lightly, the different threshold that results from a different wording of the FET clause may potentially present a problem, particularly for those countries that have subscribed to treaties using different language. The threshold for qualifying conduct by the State towards one investor, protected by one type of standard can be different from the finding of a violation with respect to another investor of a different nationality. The result would then not only be unpredictable but also contrary to the objective of investment treaties to guarantee non-discrimination.

3. The need for effective balancing of interests

A further concern about how the FET standard has evolved arises from the relationship between regulatory measures adversely affecting investors and the reasons underlying these measures. One such reason could be that the host country is under an international obligation to achieve a specific regulatory outcome, such as an international environmental, public health or human rights protection obligation. Where a government undertakes a regulatory measure in furtherance of such a commitment and results in a change to the legal or commercial environment and negatively affects investment, it is uncertain whether the tribunal will accept the nature of the measure as a response trumping an FET claim. The International Centre for Settlement of Investment Disputes (ICSID) arbitration recently initiated against Uruguay by Philip Morris, a tobacco products manufacturer, provides an illustration.[6] Philip Morris International (PMI) challenges the new rules requiring that 80% of cigarette pack surfaces be devoted to graphic warnings of the dangers associated with smoking as well as increases in tobacco taxes. From the company's perspective, it could be argued that the remainder of the package is insufficient to make its trademark visible, preventing consumers from distinguishing between different cigarette brands.[7]

Another factor relevant to ensuring a proper balance between investor and host country interests when applying the FET standard concerns host country characteristics. It has not generally been accepted by tribunals that the content of the standard should be adapted to the level of development of the host country.[8] That said, some more recent cases that discuss the concept of legitimate expectations have suggested that the conditions in the host country should play a part in the analysis of whether the standard has been breached.[9] In other words, a level of expectations on the part of the investor is correlated with the investment environment in the host country.

Conduct of the investor should also be relevant to the balancing exercise. As discussed in greater detail in section III, some tribunals recognized that unconscionable conduct by the investor in the course of obtaining an investment contract, a failure to exercise due diligence in the undertaking of the commercial feasibility study prior to making the investment and negligent management of the investment once it has been made, can all affect the chances of a successful FET claim.[10]

In short, it is necessary to draw a boundary between the genuine mistreatment of foreign investments that should be outlawed by the FET standard and measures of sovereign States taken in pursuance of legitimate policies that cannot be held in breach of the standard, even where such measures harm foreign investments. It is also necessary to develop criteria to assess the seriousness of the breach that is required for finding of a violation of the standard and to explore the possibilities for striking an effective balance between interests at the compensation stage.

Notes

[1] See *The Concise Oxford Dictionary of Current English,* Eighth edition, Clarendon Press, Oxford, 1990, p. 420.
[2] *Ibid.,* p. 396.
[3] See Brownlie, 2008, p. 25. In the *Tunisia-Libya Continental Shelf Case*, the International Court of Justice (ICJ) held that: "Application of equitable principles is to be distinguished from a decision ex aequo et bono. The Court can take such a decision only on condition that the parties agree (Art.38, para. 2 of the Statute), and the Court is then freed from the strict application of legal rules in order to bring about an appropriate settlement. The task of the Court in the present case is quite different: it is bound to apply equitable principles as part of international law and to balance up the

various considerations which it regards as relevant in order to produce an equitable result"[emphasis added], *I.C.J. Reports* 1982, 18, para. 71.

[4] Porterfield, 2006, referring to Thomas Franck's definition of a legitimate norm as the one providing reasonably clear guidance concerning the obligation that it imposes ("To be legitimate, a rule must communicate what conduct is permitted and what conduct is out of bounds.").

[5] See section III.A.2.

[6] *FTR Holding S.A. (Switzerland), Philip Morris Products S.A. (Switzerland) and Abal Hermanos S.A. (Uruguay) v. Oriental Republic of Uruguay* (ICSID Case No. ARB/10/7), registered 26 March 2010.

[7] See, for example, *Methanex v. United States,* in which the tribunal held that the regulatory and political environment may be a factor that the investor should take into account, and to anticipate regulatory change in areas where high levels of regulation can be foreseen, unless the host country has given assurances that no regulatory changes will take place. See *Methanex v. United States,* UNCITRAL, Final Award on Jurisdiction and Merits, 3 August 2005, Part IV – Chapter D, paras. 9–10. See section III.B.1.

[8] See Gallus, 2005.

[9] See section II.F.4.

[10] See section III.B.6.

II. STOCKTAKING OF TREATY PRACTICE

The vast majority of IIAs include the FET standard, although they express it in different ways. The manner in which this standard is set out in IIAs plays an important role in answering the questions relating to its scope and content. The most important distinction arises between the FET provision explicitly linked to the minimum standard of treatment under customary international law, on the one hand, and the unqualified formulation of the obligation (that is, simply an undertaking to accord fair and equitable treatment), on the other. More recent treaties have started to include some additional language clarifying the meaning of the obligation. It is crucial for States entering into IIAs to make an informed decision when making a reference to FET in one way or another.

A. Formulations of the FET standard in current treaty practice[1]

This subsection offers an overview of the currently used variations of the FET standard in treaty texts.[2] Some countries have changed their approach over time, others have not. A vast majority of countries, particularly developing countries, have treaties in force with the FET obligation expressed in several ways.

The variations in language may impact the outcome of the interpretative process. In particular, the degree of generality or specificity of the wording will affect the scope of discretion offered to an interpreting body, whether a government official, agency or an arbitral tribunal.

The most important and widespread approaches to the FET standard in treaty practice are the following:

(a) No FET obligation;

(b) FET without any reference to international law or any further criteria (referred to as unqualified, autonomous or self-standing FET standard);

(c) FET linked to international law;

(d) FET linked to the minimum standard of treatment of aliens under customary international law;

(e) FET with additional substantive content (denial of justice, unreasonable/discriminatory measures, breach of other treaty obligations, accounting for the level of development).

Existing treaty practice has examples of other types of FET clauses such as combined in one article with national treatment or most-favoured-nation treatment (MFN), for example. However, these types do not appear to be significant in conceptual terms.[3] The main listed approaches are examined in turn.

B. No FET obligation

A recent example of investment agreements with no reference to fair and equitable treatment are the IIAs entered into by Singapore.[4] Thus the Australia-Singapore FTA of 2003 emphasizes national treatment as the main standard of treatment, as does the India-Singapore Comprehensive Economic Cooperation Agreement of 2005. Other examples of IIAs that do not contain an FET clause include the New Zealand-Singapore FTA of 2001, the New Zealand-Thailand Closer Economic Partnership Agreement (EPA) (2005), the Albania-Croatia BIT (1993), the Croatia-Ukraine BIT (1997) and a number of BITs concluded by Turkey.

Silence on fair and equitable treatment may well indicate that the States parties to the agreement are unwilling to subject their regulatory measures to review under this standard. However, despite the absence of the FET obligation in a treaty, the international minimum standard still exists in customary law. The question is whether an investor would be able to enforce the minimum standard of treatment of aliens through an IIA's investor-State dispute settlement (ISDS) mechanism. This will depend on the breadth of the treaty's ISDS clause. For instance, the ISDS clause in the India-

Singapore Comprehensive Economic Cooperation Agreement applies only to disputes "concerning an alleged breach of an obligation of the former under this Chapter" (Article 6.21); therefore, given the absence of the FET clause in the treaty, claims alleging breaches of the minimum standard of treatment of aliens will fall outside the tribunal's jurisdiction. In contrast, the New Zealand-Thailand Closer Economic Partnership Agreement's arbitration clause encompasses all disputes "with respect to a covered investment" (Article 9.16) – there is no requirement that relevant claims arise from a violation of the Agreement itself. Such a clause is broad enough to include, among others, claims of violation of the minimum standard of treatment of aliens under customary international law.

Another possibility is that the FET standard could be read into the treaty by way of the MFN clause. In the *Bayindir* case, the tribunal did accept the MFN argument. This case concerned, among other matters, the question as to whether the claimant, a Turkish road construction company, could invoke the FET standard even though it was absent from the text of the Pakistan-Turkey BIT (the claim alleged a breach of the FET standard by the Pakistani authorities due to the termination of the claimants' involvement in a major motorway construction project). The tribunal held that the reference to the FET standard in the preamble of the Pakistan-Turkey BIT (1995) allowed use of the MFN clause to import that standard from Pakistan's BIT with a third party:

"It is true that the reference to FET in the preamble together with the absence of a FET clause in the Treaty might suggest that Turkey and Pakistan intended not to include an FET obligation in the Treaty. The Tribunal is, however, not persuaded that this suggestion rules out the possibility of importing an FET obligation through the MFN clause expressly included in the Treaty. The fact that the States parties to the Treaty clearly contemplated the importance of the FET rather suggests the contrary. Indeed, even though it does not establish

an operative obligation, the preamble is relevant for the interpretation of the MFN clause in its context and in the light of the Treaty's object and purpose pursuant to Article 31(1) of the VCLT [Vienna Convention on the Law of Treaties]."

The MFN clause has also been used to incorporate the FET obligation from a third-party treaty in other cases.[5]

Treaty practice suggests that countries that have not included an FET obligation or a reference to it into their treaty have done so purposefully to avoid being exposed to this standard of protection. Accordingly, any introduction of an FET clause from another IIA through the MFN clause should be done with care and take into account the clear intention of the parties (UNCTAD, 2010a, p. 102).

C. Unqualified FET formulation

Many IIAs use a simple unqualified formulation which does no more than state the obligation of a host State to accord fair and equitable treatment to protected investments (box 1).

Box 1. Belgium-Luxembourg Economic Union-Tajikistan BIT (2009)

Article 3

All investments made by investors of one Contracting Party shall enjoy a fair and equitable treatment in the territory of the other Contracting Party.

In some agreements – especially in Spanish and French language treaties – the phrase appears as "just and equitable treatment". This variation appears to be interchangeable with "fair and equitable treatment" and can be directly translated as such from French ("un traitement juste et equitable") or Spanish ("un trato justo y equitativo").

Some agreements use the unqualified form of the FET standard and link it with the standard of full protection and security in the same clause (box 2).

Box 2. China-Switzerland BIT (2009)

Article 4

Investments and returns of investors of either Contracting Party shall at all times be accorded fair and equitable treatment and shall enjoy full protection and security in the territory of the other Contracting Party.

Such a formulation would not modify the interpretation of the FET standard; it merely lists both standards of treatment in the same provision.

The unqualified approach has given rise to the question of whether the FET clause formulated in this way can be interpreted in the light of the minimum standard of treatment of aliens under customary law or whether it refers to an unqualified autonomous standard that can be interpreted on a case-by-case basis by reference to general notions of fairness and equity. On the one hand, there is evidence suggesting that even an unqualified FET obligation should be equated to the minimum standard of treatment under customary law. In particular, the commentary to the 1967 OECD Draft Convention on the Protection of Foreign Property, which included an unqualified FET formulation, equated FET to the minimum standard.[6] This understanding was further confirmed in 1984 when the OECD Committee on International Investment and Multinational Enterprises reported, "[a]ccording to all Member countries which have commented on this point, fair and equitable treatment introduced a substantive legal standard referring to general principles of international law even if this is not explicitly stated."[7] Even though the draft convention served as a blueprint for many countries' bilateral investment treaties, it remained a text without legal effect. Neither does the 1984 OECD report have a binding force. These factors may have influenced many arbitral tribunals that interpreted the unqualified FET standard as delinked from customary international law and focused on the plain meaning of the terms "fair" and "equitable".

As discussed in section I.B, such an interpretation leaves a wide margin of discretion to arbitrators and may lead to an overbroad and surprising extension of the FET standard towards the review of wide categories of governmental action previously regarded as being outside the remit of international law review. The simple unqualified formulation may result in a low liability threshold and brings with it a risk for State regulatory action to be found in breach of it.

D. FET linked to international law

FET clauses in IIAs display two types of reference to international law. The first type is illustrated in box 3.

Box 3. Croatia-Oman BIT (2004)

Article 3(2)

[...]

*2. Investments or returns of investors of either Contracting Party in the territory of the other Contracting Party shall be accorded fair and equitable treatment **in accordance with international law** and provisions of this Agreement.* [Emphasis added]

This formulation prevents the use of a purely semantic approach to the interpretation of the FET standard and is meant to ensure that the interpreter uses principles of international law, including, but not limited to, customary international law. Indeed a tribunal faced with such language may not go beyond what the sources of international law dictate the scope and meaning of FET to be. It requires a review of the sources to ascertain whether a specific claim that a State's conduct breaches fair and equitable treatment is justified. General principles of law derived from national legal systems may prove useful in analysing the scope of the relevant FET obligations (Schill, 2010). The process of discerning such principles can be laborious, but it will advance the understanding of the FET content.

The second type of the FET clause linked to international law is illustrated in box 4.

Box 4. Bahrain-United States BIT (1999)

Article 2(3)(a)

*Each Party shall at all times accord to covered investments fair and equitable treatment and full protection and security, **and shall in no case accord treatment less favorable than that required by international law**.* [Emphasis added]

In this formulation, the FET obligation is not strictly linked to the stipulations of international law. Rather, international law here appears to set the floor of protection that can be claimed by an investor.[8] The FET obligation cannot go below that floor but, judging from the text alone, it would seem to give more room for interpreting FET as adding to the international law requirements. Such a formulation is thus effectively closer to the unqualified FET standard and gives arbitrators greater freedom of interpretation.

E. FET linked to the minimum standard under customary international law

An increasing number of IIAs link the FET obligation to the minimum standard of treatment of aliens (MST) under customary international law. The relationship between fair and equitable treatment and customary international law has been at the heart of the NAFTA debate. Under Article 1105(1) of the NAFTA "Minimum Standard of Treatment", each Party committed to "accord to investments of investors of another Party **treatment in accordance with international law, including fair and equitable treatment** and full protection and security" [emphasis added]. This formulation gave rise to concerns among the Contracting Parties after the NAFTA arbitration tribunal in *Pope and Talbot v. Canada* ruled that the FET standard was "additive" to the international minimum standard.[9] Following that arbitral award, the NAFTA Free Trade Commission, composed of representatives of the three NAFTA countries, issued in 2001 the Notes of Interpretation, which rejected any notion that NAFTA Article 1105 contained any elements that were "additive" to the international minimum standard (box 5).

Box 5. NAFTA Free Trade Commission: Notes of interpretation of certain Chapter 11 provisions, 31 July 2001

Minimum Standard of Treatment in Accordance with International Law

Article 1105(1) prescribes the customary international law minimum standard of treatment of aliens as the minimum standard of treatment to be afforded to investments of investors of another Party.

The concepts of "fair and equitable treatment" and "full protection and security" do not require treatment in addition to or beyond that which is required by the customary international law minimum standard of treatment of aliens.

A determination that there has been a breach of another provision of the NAFTA, or of a separate international agreement, does not establish that there has been a breach of Article 1105(1).

Source:
http://www.sice.oas.org/tpd/nafta/Commission/CH11understanding_e.asp.

The language of the NAFTA Free Trade Commission's Note has found its way into the subsequent model BITs of the NAFTA countries. It has also has been echoed in a significant and growing number of recent IIAs involving non-NAFTA countries, including the Agreement Establishing the ASEAN-Australia-New Zealand Free Trade Area (2009), the Japan-Philippines FTA (2006), the China-Peru FTA (2009), the Malaysia-New Zealand FTA (2009), the India-Republic of Korea Comprehensive Economic Partnership Agreement (2009) and others (see examples in box 6).

Box 6. Examples of provisions with a reference to the customary international law minimum standard of treatment

Agreement Establishing the ASEAN-Australia-New Zealand Free Trade Area (2009)

Chapter 11, Article 6

Treatment of Investment

1. Each Party shall accord to covered investments fair and equitable treatment and full protection and security.

2. For greater certainty:

(a) fair and equitable treatment requires each Party not to deny justice in any legal or administrative proceedings;

(b) full protection and security requires each Party to take such measures as may be reasonably necessary to ensure the protection and security of the covered investment; and

*(c) **the concepts of "fair and equitable treatment" and "full protection and security" do not require treatment in addition to or beyond that which is required under customary** international law, and do not create additional substantive rights.*

/...

Box 6 (concluded)

3. A determination that there has been a breach of another provision of this Agreement, or of a separate international agreement, does not establish that there has been a breach of this Article. [Emphasis added]

Source: http://www.aseansec.org/22260.pdf

Agreement between Japan and the Republic of the Philippines for an Economic Partnership (2006)

Article 91: General Treatment

*Each Party shall accord to investments of investors of the other Party **treatment in accordance with international law, including fair and equitable treatment** and full protection and security.*

Note: ***This Article prescribes the customary international law minimum standard of treatment of aliens as the minimum standard of treatment to be afforded to investments of investors of the other Party. The concepts of "fair and equitable treatment" and "full protection and security" do not require treatment in addition to or beyond that which is required by the customary international law minimum standard of treatment of aliens.*** *A determination that there has been a breach of another provision of this Agreement, or of a separate international agreement, does not ipso facto establish that there has been a breach of this Article.* [Emphasis added]

Source: http://www.mofa.go.jp/region/asia-paci/philippine/epa0609/index.html.

The alignment of the FET standard with the MST is also further developed in the recent IIAs of the United States (box 7) and Canada, and in FTAs of the western hemisphere.[10] Recent IIAs concluded by the United States not only incorporate the NAFTA Interpretative Note approach, but also add that FET includes the obligation not to deny justice. In addition, they have a separate annex that explains that the term "customary international law" in the FET clause refers to all principles of customary international law for the protection of the economic rights and interests of aliens.

Box 7. Rwanda-United States BIT (2008)

Article 5: Minimum Standard of Treatment[9]

1. *Each Party shall accord to covered investments treatment in accordance with customary international law, including fair and equitable treatment and full protection and security.*

2. *For greater certainty, paragraph 1 prescribes the customary international law minimum standard of treatment of aliens as the minimum standard of treatment to be afforded to covered investments. The concepts of "fair and equitable treatment" and "full protection and security" do not require treatment in addition to or beyond that which is required by that standard, and do not create additional substantive rights. The obligation in paragraph 1 to provide:*

(a) *"fair and equitable treatment" includes the obligation not to deny justice in criminal, civil, or administrative adjudicatory proceedings in accordance with the principle of due process embodied in the principal legal systems of the world; and*

(b) *"full protection and security" requires each Party to provide the level of police protection required under customary international law.*

3. *A determination that there has been a breach of another provision of this Treaty, or of a separate international agreement, does not establish that there has been a breach of this Article.*

[9] *Article 5 shall be interpreted in accordance with Annex A.*

/...

Box 7 (concluded)

Annex A

Customary International Law

The Parties confirm their shared understanding that "customary international law" generally and as specifically referenced in Article 5 and Annex B results from a general and consistent practice of States that they follow from a sense of legal obligation. With regard to Article 5, the customary international law minimum standard of treatment of aliens refers to all customary international law principles that protect the economic rights and interests of aliens.

An explicit link between the FET obligation and the minimum standard of treatment is used in these treaties to prevent overexpansive interpretations of the FET standard by arbitral tribunals and to further guide them by referring to an example of gross misconduct that would violate the minimum standard of treatment of aliens – denial of justice. By limiting the source of FET to customary international law, these treaties seek to rein in the discretion of tribunals when considering its content. In other words, treaties incorporating a reference to the minimum standard of treatment of aliens under customary law send out a message to arbitrators that the latter cannot go beyond what customary international law declares to be the content of the minimum standard of treatment.

The difficulty with this line of thinking is that it presupposes the existence of a general consensus as to what constitutes the minimum standard of treatment of aliens under customary international law. The reality, however, is that the minimum standard itself is highly indeterminate, lacks a clearly defined content and requires interpretation.[11] The process of establishing the content of customary international law (determining State practice and opinio juris) is methodologically difficult and puts an onerous burden on the claimants. As discussed in section III.A, existing awards of arbitral tribunals do not share a common approach to the interpretation of the clauses relating to fair and equitable treatment and the minimum standard of treatment of aliens; thus, a degree of unpredictability persists, despite the attempted clarifications in the treaties. Nevertheless, from the host country perspective, linking the FET standard to the minimum standard of treatment of aliens may be seen as a progressive step, given that this will likely lead tribunals to apply a higher threshold for finding a breach of the standard, as compared with unqualified FET clauses.

F. FET with additional substantive content

An emerging trend in IIA rule making is to add substantive content to FET clauses. This is also a way of being more precise about the content of the FET obligation and more predictable in its implementation and subsequent interpretation. Indeed, the more specific the clause, the clearer its scope and content. This section reviews some formulations in existing treaty practice under the following headings:

(a) Prohibition of denial of justice;

(b) Prohibition of arbitrary, unreasonable or discriminatory measures;

(c) Irrelevance of a breach of a different treaty norm;

(d) Accounting for the level of development.

1. Prohibition of denial of justice

A number of recent IIAs have expressly included a reference to a denial of justice in their FET clause. This has been done in two ways. More often, one can encounter a clause that says that FET includes the obligation not to deny justice in legal or administrative proceedings (see examples in boxes 6 and 7). The word "includes" indicates that the obligation not to deny justice forms part of the FET standard but that the latter is not limited to the denial of justice only; it may include other elements as well. These provisions – in addition to specifically mentioning the denial of justice – typically also refer to the minimum standard of treatment of aliens, which is a broader notion. At the same time, a reference to the denial of justice, which outlaws only the gravest instances of injustice (see section III.B.3), may be taken to indicate that a breach of another aspect of the FET standard (prohibition of arbitrariness, discrimination and so forth) may be established only if such violation is equally severe.

The second type of this clause is illustrated in box 8.

Box 8. ASEAN Comprehensive Investment Agreement (2009)

Article 11

Treatment of Investment

1. Each Member State shall accord to covered investments of investors of any other Member State, fair and equitable treatment and full protection and security.

2. For greater certainty:

*(a) fair and equitable treatment **requires** each Member State not to deny justice in any legal or administrative proceedings in accordance with the principle of due process...* [Emphasis added]

Source: http://www.aseansec.org/22260.pdf

The language used here may be read to suggest that the FET standard is limited to the denial of justice, as it states that "treatment requires" rather than "includes".[12] Even more clearly, the ASEAN-China Investment Agreement (2009) states that FET "refers to the obligation not to deny justice [...]". Notably, neither the ASEAN agreement, nor the ASEAN-China agreement refer to the minimum standard under customary international law, which gives additional support to the conclusion that the FET obligation is limited to the obligation not to deny justice and does not encompass other protections that may exist in the minimum standard of treatment of aliens.

2. Prohibition of arbitrary, unreasonable and discriminatory measures

Some treaties, after setting out the general FET standard, specifically prohibit arbitrary, unreasonable or discriminatory measures (see box 9).[13] The notion of arbitrariness, unreasonableness and discrimination are intrinsic to the FET standard (see section III.B). Thus, it may be said that such clauses give some further substance to the otherwise general wording of the standard.

Prohibiting arbitrary or unreasonable measures, in addition to laying down the general FET standard (as done in treaties reproduced in box 9) does not help delineate the scope of the general FET standard. The prohibition of unreasonable, arbitrary and/or discriminatory measures is consonant with the FET standard, but the standard itself goes beyond this prohibition. Some arbitral tribunals have found a State measure to be not unreasonable, not arbitrary and non-discriminatory, but nevertheless a violation of the FET standard. For example, in *LG&E v. Argentina*, the tribunal concluded that "the charges imposed by Argentina to Claimants' investment, though unfair and inequitable, were the result of reasoned judgment rather than simple disregard of the rule of law" and refused to hold them arbitrary.[14] Thus, the general FET standard, in its application and interpretation, has been considered to be broader than the notions of arbitrariness, unreasonableness and discrimination.

In light of this, if a State wishes to restrict the scope of the FET clause to the prohibition of arbitrariness, unreasonable conduct or discrimination – or possibly certain other types of conduct such as the denial of justice – it may wish to replace a general FET standard with a qualified provision including these specific prohibitions (see policy option 4 in section IV).

Box 9. FET provisions referring to arbitrary, unreasonable and/or discriminatory treatment

Netherlands-Oman BIT (2009)

Article 2(2)

[...]

2) Each Contracting Party shall ensure fair and equitable treatment to the investments or nationals or persons of the other Contracting Party and shall not impair, by unjustified or discriminatory measures, the operation, management, maintenance, use, enjoyment or disposal thereof by those nationals or persons.

Romania-United States BIT (1994)

Article II(2)

[...]

2. (a) Investment shall at all times be accorded fair and equitable treatment, shall enjoy full protection and security and shall in no case be accorded treatment less than that required by international law.

(b) Neither Party shall in any way impair by arbitrary or discriminatory measures the management, operation, maintenance, use, enjoyment, acquisition, expansion, or disposal of investments.

---

3. Irrelevance of a breach of a different treaty norm

Following the issuance of the 2001 interpretative note by the NAFTA Free Trade Commission (see box 5), some IIAs started to include an explicit clarification that the breach of another provision in the IIA or a breach of another international agreement by a contracting party will not by itself constitute a breach of the FET standard. Box 10 provides an example.

Box 10. Mexico-Singapore BIT (2009)

Article 4(3)

A determination that there has been a breach of another provision of this Agreement, or of a separate international agreement, does not establish that there has been a breach of this Article.

Indeed, if FET is understood as part of the minimum standard of treatment under customary international law, it becomes clear that a violation of a treaty obligation does not necessarily amount to a violation of a customary norm. The purpose of this provision is to prevent tribunals from automatically finding a breach of the FET standard when another provision in the IIA has been breached, as happened in the *SD Myers v. Canada* case under NAFTA.[15]

This clarification appears to be particularly important with respect to non-IIA treaty obligations (such as World Trade Organization (WTO) law). Those other international instruments may lack private enforcement mechanisms that exist in IIAs. If investors could automatically establish violations of the FET standard on the basis of, for example, a host State's breaches of WTO law, this would expose host governments to the risk of numerous suits accompanied by compensation claims under the investment chapter of an FTA or a BIT.

4. Accounting for the level of development

Another issue that has received attention and has been addressed recently in one treaty is that the finding of an FET violation must take into account the level of development of the host country (see box 11).

Box 11. Investment Agreement for the COMESA Common Investment Area (2007)

Article 14 (3)

For greater certainty, Member States understand that different Member States have different forms of administrative, legislative and judicial systems and that Member States at different levels of development may not achieve the same standards at the same time. Paragraphs 1 and 2 of this Article [prohibition of the denial of justice and affirmation of the minimum standard of treatment of aliens] *do not establish a single international standard in this context.*

This language is meant to introduce flexibility in the interpretation of the FET standard based on the level of development of the respondent country. This acknowledges the reality of doing business in less developed countries, which often includes a less than optimal level of functioning of public administration. It would be unreasonable for investors in developing countries, let alone least developed countries, to have expectations of treatment by the local authorities no different from that anticipated in the most advanced countries. It may thus be argued that even in the absence of specific language, the level of development of the host-country institutions should be taken into account, as it clearly has an impact on what the investor may legitimately expect from the State authorities in terms of their efficiency and conduct.[16] The commitment of a State to grant fair and equitable treatment may thus be read differently, depending on what is reasonable to expect from a particular State in its particular situation. Article 14 of the COMESA Agreement explicitly requires that tribunals take into account particularities of local governance practices in their interpretation of fair and equitable treatment. This kind of flexibility does not exist where the FET standard is equated with the minimum standard of treatment of aliens, as the latter itself is "a floor, an absolute bottom, below which conduct is not accepted by the international community" and which "is not meant to vary from state to state".[17]

* * *

In sum, a number of treaties clarify the meaning of the FET standard by mentioning some elements or aspects of its substantive content. This approach appears to be a step in the right direction; it could be further developed by replacing the FET standard with more specific obligations (see policy option 4 in section IV) or by formulating the requirements included in the standard in the form of an exhaustive list.

Notes

[1] Unless indicated otherwise, the texts of international investment agreements mentioned in the paper can be found in UNCTAD's databases at www.unctad.org/iia.

[2] Given that many IIAs mention the FET standard together with the obligation to accord full protection and security to investments, it needs to be clarified that the two standards cover distinctive areas. FET deals with the process of administrative and judicial decision-making, while the full protection standard is usually understood as the obligation for the host State to adopt all reasonable measures to physically protect assets and property from threats or attacks by public officials or third parties. Accordingly this standard will not inform the FET standard as such.

[3] For a review of the relevant treaty practice and examples, see UNCTAD 2007, pp. 28–33.

[4] Australia-Singapore FTA (2003); New Zealand-Singapore FTA (2009); India-Singapore Comprehensive Economic Cooperation Agreement (2005).

[5] *Rumeli Telekom v. Kazakhstan*, ICSID Case No. ARB/05/16, Award, 29 July 2008, para. 575. (The applicable Turkey-Kazakhstan BIT did not have the FET clause, but the respondent agreed to the incorporation of the FET standard, alongside some other substantive protections, from the Kazakhstan-United Kingdom BIT); *ATA Construction v. Jordan*, ICSID Case No. ARB/08/2, Award, 18 May 2010, footnote 16 to para.125. (The Jordan-Turkey BIT was the applicable BIT, the FET clause was incorporated from the Jordan-United Kingdom BIT.)

[6] "The phrase "fair and equitable treatment", customary in relevant bilateral agreements, indicates the standard set by international law for the treatment due by each State with regard to the property of foreign nationals. [...] *The standard required conforms in effect to the "minimum standard" which forms part of customary international law.*" [Emphasis added; OECD, 1967, p. 120.]

[7] OECD, 1984, p. 12, para. 36.

[8] Such was the interpretation given to this type of clause by tribunals in *Azurix v. Argentina*, ICSID Case No. ARB/01/12, Award, 4 July 2006, para. 361; *Duke Energy v. Ecuador*, ICSID Case No. ARB/04/19, Award,

18 August 2008, para. 337; and *Lemire v. Ukraine*, ICSID Case No. ARB(AF)/98/1, Decision on Jurisdiction and Liability, 21 January 2010, para. 253.

[9] See *Pope and Talbot v. Canada*, UNCITRAL, Award on the Merits of Phase 2, 10 April 2001, para. 110.

[10] See for example Dominican Republic-Central America-United States Free Trade Agreement (CAFTA-DR) of 2004, Article 10.5.

[11] See Porterfield, 2006, p. 88. See section III.A.1 for a more detailed discussion.

[12] The formulation using the word "requires" can also be found in Article 10.10 of the Malaysia-New Zealand FTA (2009) and Article 6 of the ASEAN-Australia-New Zealand Free Trade Agreement.

[13] The relevant language has its origin in the 1959 Abs-Shawcross Draft Convention on Investments Abroad and is repeated in the 1967 OECD Draft Convention on the Protection of Foreign Property. Both texts set out a general FET standard and additionally prohibit impairment of property through unreasonable or discriminatory measures.

[14] *LG&E v. Argentina*, ICSID Case No. ARB/02/1, Decision on Liability, 3 October 2006, para. 162. See also *Sempra Energy v. Argentina*, ICSID Case No. ARB/02/16, Award, 28 September 2007, paras. 318–320; *Enron v. Argentina*, ICSID Case No. ARB/01/3, Award, 22 May 2007, paras. 281–283; *PSEG v. Turkey*, ICSID Case No. ARB/02/5, Award, 19 January 2007, para. 262; and *Duke Energy v. Ecuador*, ICSID Case No. ARB/04/19, Award, 18 August 2008, paras. 380–383.

[15] In this case, the majority of the tribunal held that having breached NAFTA's provision on national treatment, Canada had also breached the minimum standard of treatment.

[16] On the existing arbitral practice on this issue, see section III.B.1.

[17] *Glamis Gold, Ltd. v. United States*, UNCITRAL (NAFTA), Award, 8 June 2009, para. 615.

III. INVESTOR-STATE ARBITRAL PRACTICE

The FET standard has been considered in numerous cases. Claims based on the standard appear practically in every single treaty-based arbitration proceeding. They have been both accepted and rejected in significant numbers by tribunals (see box 15).

A wide range of governmental actions has been considered in these cases. Box 12 illustrates the types of State conduct challenged by investors as inconsistent with the FET standard.

Box 12. Illustrative list of the types of State conduct challenged by investors as violating the FET obligation

Some of these claims were accepted and others rejected by tribunals.

Measures relating to business operations:

- Revocation or refusal to renew an operating licence:
    - *Wena Hotels Ltd. v. Egypt*, ICSID Case No. ARB/98/4;
    - *Genin v. Estonia*, ICSID Case No. ARB/99/2;
    - *Tecmed v. Mexico*, ICSID Case No. ARB (AF)/00/2);

- Refusal to issue a permit required for business operations:
    - *Metalclad v. Mexico*, ICSID Case No. ARB(AF)/97/1;
    - *MTD v. Chile*, ICSID Case No. ARB/01/7;
    - *Lemire v. Ukraine*, ICSID Case No. ARB(AF)/98/1);

- Closure of investor's business as a result of outlawing the business activity by new administration
    - *Thunderbird v. Mexico*, UNCITRAL Rules (NAFTA);

/...

Box 12 (continued)

- Closure of the State border for the movement of a certain chemical compound:
    o *Myers v. Canada*, UNCITRAL Rules (NAFTA);
- Ban on manufacturing and selling of products that contained a certain substance:
    o *Methanex v. United States*, UNCITRAL Rules (NAFTA);
- Regulatory review and eventual phase out of pesticide business:
    o *Chemtura v. Canada*, UNCITRAL Rules (NAFTA).

Introducing requirements that hinder economic performance of an investment:

- Limitation of the amount of products that the claimant can export:
    o *Pope & Talbot Inc. v. Canada*, UNCITRAL Rules (NAFTA);
- Forcing the investor to source its raw material from local sources :
    o *ADF Group Inc. v. United States*, ICSID Case No. ARB (AF)/00/1;
- Requirements related to backfilling and grading for mining operations in the vicinity of sensitive sites:
    o *Glamis Gold, Ltd. v. United States*, UNCITRAL Rules (NAFTA);
- Changes of quotas for producers
    o *Eastern Sugar B.V. v. Czech Republic*, SCC Case No. 088/2004);
- Discriminatory refusal to provide financial assistance:
    o *Saluka v. Czech Republic*, UNCITRAL Rules

/...

Box 12 (continued)

- Withdrawal of tax exemptions:
    - *Biwater v. Tanzania*, ICSID Case No. ARB/05/22;
- Refusal to reimburse VAT in violation of the investment contract:
    - *Occidental v. Ecuador*, LCIA Case No. UN3467;
- Changing the monetary parity system
    - *Continental Casualty v. Argentina*, ICSID Case No. ARB/03/9;
    - *Metalpar v. Argentina*, ICSID Case No. ARB/03/5;
- Suspension of tariff adjustments for public utilities:
    - *CMS v. Argentina*, ICSID Case No. ARB/01/8;
    - *Enron v. Argentina*, ICSID Case No. ARB/01/3;
    - *Sempra Energy v. Argentina*, ICSID Case No. ARB/02/16;
    - *LG&E v. Argentina*, ICSID Case No. ARB/02/1.

Interference with contractual rights:

- Unilateral termination of an investment contract:
    - *Rumeli Telekom v. Kazakhstan*, ICSID Case No. ARB/05/16;
    - *Helnan v. Egypt*, ICSID Case No. ARB/05/19;
    - *M.C.I. Power v. Ecuador*, ICSID Case No. ARB/03/6;
    - *Siemens v. Argentina*, ICSID Case No. ARB/02/8;
    - *Parkerings-Compagniet AS v. Lithuania*, ICSID Case No. ARB/05/8;
    - *Azinian v. Mexico*, ICSID Case No. ARB (AF)/97/2;
    - *Bayindir v. Pakistan*, ICSID Case No. ARB/03/29;

- Declining to renew an investment contract:
    - *EDF v. Romania*, ICSID Case No. ARB/05/13;

/...

Box 12 (continued)

- Breach of an investment contract by the State:
    - *Mondev v. United States*, ICSID Case No. ARB(AF)/99/2;
    - *Duke Energy v. Ecuador,* ICSID Case No ARB/04/19;
    - *Waste Management v. Mexico*, ICSID Case No. ARB(AF)/00/3;

- Disagreements over contractually fixed tariffs:
    - *Azurix v. Argentina*, ICSID Case No. ARB/01/12;
    - *Vivendi v. Argentina*, ICSID Case No. ARB/97/3.

Interference with ownership rights:

- Physical seizure of investor's assets:
    - *Biwater v. Tanzania*, ICSID Case No. ARB/05/22;
    - *Middle East Cement v. Egypt*, ICSID Case No. ARB/99/6;

- Failure to complete the privatization process of a company:
    - *Eureko B.V. v. Republic of Poland*, ad hoc arbitration.

Abusive treatment of an investor:

- Arrests of the investor's employees and family members, imposition of an unfavourable agreement under physical and financial duress:
    - *Desert Line Projects v. Yemen*, ICSID Case No. ARB/05/17;

- Continuous interference with activities and management of investment by State tax authority:
    - *Tokios Tokelės v. Ukraine*, ICSID Case No. ARB/02/18;

/...

Box 12 (concluded)

- Political statements against foreign investment/investors:
  - *Biwater v. Tanzania*, ICSID Case No. ARB/05/22;
  - *Vivendi v. Argentina*, ICSID Case No. ARB/97/3.

Denial of justice:

- Miscarriage of justice by domestic courts:
  - *Loewen v. United States*, ICSID Case No. ARB(AF)/98/3;
  - *Azinian v. Mexico*, ICSID Case No. ARB (AF)/97/2;

- Delay in judicial proceedings and other violations of due process:
  - *Jan de Nul v. Egypt*, ICSID Case No. ARB/04/13;
  - *Amto v. Ukraine, SCC Case No. 080/2005;*
  - *Petrobart v. Kyrgyz Republic,* UNCITRAL Rules.

Existing arbitral decisions show that the range of factual situations that could conceivably give rise to arguments about their unfairness or inequity is practically limitless. The major challenge is to understand this growing number of awards, find common strands and directions in cases that would shed light on the meaning of the FET obligation and identify whether particular treaty formulations affect arbitral interpretation. This process should help, among others, to identify implications for the negotiation of FET clauses in new IIAs.

The analysis and interpretation in recent arbitral awards of the FET obligation is divided into two related parts. Section A deals with the relationship between the FET standard, as is expressed in various IIAs and the minimum standard of treatment under customary international law. Section B seeks to identify emerging substantive content of the obligation to provide fair and equitable treatment.

A. Relationship between the FET standard and the minimum standard of treatment

This section considers the relationship between the FET standard and the minimum standard of treatment of aliens under customary international law (MST). It starts by briefly considering the main sources and content of the MST. It then examines cases arbitrated under NAFTA Article 1105, as interpreted in 2001 by the NAFTA Free Trade Commission, which understands FET as a constituent element of the MST. It subsequently looks at tribunals' decisions that have applied other types of FET clauses where the standard is not linked to the MST. The concluding subsection explores the possibility of convergence of the variously expressed FET standards.

1. The international minimum standard of treatment

The MST is referred to in a number of FET clauses (see section II.E). It is a set of customary international law norms that governs the treatment of aliens. States, regardless of their legislation and practices, must respect these norms when dealing with foreign nationals and their property. The MST is often understood as a broad concept intended to encompass the doctrine of denial of justice along with other aspects of the law of State responsibility for injuries to aliens. However, specific meaning of the concept is still rather indeterminate.

Under the existing definition, customary international law results from a general and consistent practice of States that they follow from a sense of legal obligation (opinio juris). It is difficult to comply with this definition, particularly in relation to such an underdeveloped concept as the minimum standard of treatment of aliens, and a specific category of aliens – investors (economic actors) and their property. At the same time, a tribunal constituted to resolve an investor-State dispute and the disputing parties must grapple with the problem of the MST's content, if the applicable IIA requires it to do so. Given that claimants bear the burden of proof, they face the daunting task of collecting evidence in order to demonstrate general State practice and opinio juris. As discussed below, tribunals have interpreted the MST in a variety of ways, some more strict and conservative, others more creative and liberal (see next section).

An OECD report has concluded that the international minimum standard applies in the following areas: (a) the administration of justice, usually linked to the notion of the denial of justice; (b) the treatment of aliens under detention; and (c) full protection and security (OECD, 2004, p. 9, note 34). On this view, there are no other aspects of the MST that have become apparent to date in customary international law.

The most cited expression of the MST is found in the 1926 decision in *LFH Neer and Pauline Neer (United States v. Mexico)*. In that case, a claim was brought before the Mexico-United States General Claims Commission alleging that the Mexican authorities had failed to exercise due diligence in finding and prosecuting the murderer of a United States national and so had committed a denial of justice. The Commission rejected the claim, having set a high threshold of State responsibility limited to egregious acts of failure to protect the rights of aliens. The Commission stated:

*"Without attempting to announce a precise formula, it is in the opinion of the Commission possible to [...] hold (first) that the propriety of governmental acts should be put to the test of international standards, and (second) that **the treatment of an alien, in order to constitute an international delinquency, should amount to an outrage, to bad faith, to wilful neglect of***

duty, or to an insufficiency of governmental action so far short of international standards that every reasonable and impartial man would readily recognize its insufficiency. Whether the insufficiency proceeds from deficient execution of an intelligent law or from the fact that the laws of the country do not empower the authorities to measure up to international standards is immaterial."[1]

This test is directed at extremes of governmental conduct. Other relevant decisions and academic commentary on MST also emphasize "a degree of forbearance on the part of the international tribunal", which should require "convincing evidence of a pronounced degree of improper governmental action", "an obvious error in the administration of justice, or fraud or a clear outrage" (Thomas, 2002, pp. 22–38). In other words, at least in the first half of the twentieth century, the minimum standard was perceived as not very stringent or exacting on States and the liability threshold was rather high.

It must be noted that the *Neer* claim and other similar claims concerned the treatment of natural persons, and concentrated on denial of justice (Paparinskis, 2009, p. 38). Some authors made general statements that MST also protects the property of aliens (Roth, 1949, p. 186; Jennings and Watts, 1996, p. 912) but the extent of such protection or the applicable legal tests, short of a prohibition of an uncompensated expropriation of property, have not been well developed prior to the inclusion of the FET standard coupled with the MST into investment treaties (see Sornarajah, 2010, p. 347).

The MST is a concept that does not offer ready-made solutions for deciding modern investment disputes; at best, it gives a rough idea of a high threshold that the challenged governmental conduct has to meet for a breach to be established. In fact, the contemporary practice of arbitral tribunals and discussions within the broader investment community helps to flesh out the minimum standard of treatment of foreign investors and their investments.

2. NAFTA awards addressing the minimum standard of treatment

As noted in section II, prior to the Interpretative Note of the NAFTA Free Trade Commission, the tribunal in the *Pope & Talbot v. Canada* case asserted that the FET standard was "additive" to the minimum standard of treatment of aliens and so tribunals were free to go beyond the limits of the latter, thereby rejecting the argument of Canada that the standard required a finding of egregious misconduct in accordance with the standard developed in the *Neer* case. One of the first NAFTA tribunals to address the meaning of Article 1105, in *Myers v. Canada*, took a deferential stance towards sovereign acts and set a rather high liability threshold. In 2000, it held that Article 1105 could be breached:

> "[O]nly *when it is shown that an investor has been treated in such an unjust or arbitrary manner that the treatment rises to the level that is* **unacceptable from the international perspective.** *That determination must be made in the light of the* **high measure of deference that international law generally extends to the right of domestic authorities to regulate matters within their own borders.** *The determination must also take into account any specific rules of international law that are applicable to the case."*[2]

As discussed in section II.E, in the wake of controversy over another early decision, in *Pope & Talbot v. Canada*, the NAFTA Free Trade Commission issued its 2001 Interpretative Note, whereby it clarified that fair and equitable treatment did not "require treatment in addition to or beyond that which is required by the customary international law minimum standard of treatment of aliens". Arbitral awards issued shortly thereafter sought to follow the Free Trade Commission's clarification but interpreted the MST in an evolutionary way. For example in *Mondev v. United States* and *ADF v. United States,* the tribunals held that NAFTA's FET standard included the *Neer* standard, but that it had evolved over time going beyond the types of egregious misconduct referred to in *Neer,* though in neither case was a violation of Article 1105(1) established (box 13).

Box 13. NAFTA tribunal awards after the Interpretative Note of the NAFTA Free Trade Commission

Mondev International Ltd v. United States, ICSID Case
No. ARB (AF)/99/2, Award, 11 October 2002

In this case Mondev, a Canadian property developer, brought, through its local subsidiary, a claim against the City of Boston and the Boston Redevelopment Authority for breach of a contract. On appeal, the Massachusetts courts held that the Boston Redevelopment Authority was immune from suit under the law of State immunity. Mondev then brought a claim under Article 1105(1) of NAFTA arguing that it had suffered a denial of justice in breach of the FET provision. The tribunal did not uphold the claim on the principal ground that the Massachusetts courts had applied domestic law correctly. Its remarks concerning the FET, MST and the *Neer* standard can be summarized as follows:

- The *Neer* case and other similar cases concerned "not the treatment of foreign investment as such but the physical security of the alien";

- In the *Neer* case, the alleged State responsibility arose of the failure of Mexico to prosecute private parties whose acts had been out of control of Mexico – in such cases a State can be held responsible only in special circumstances;

- It cannot be assumed that NAFTA is confined to the *Neer*

/...

Box 13 (continued)

standard of outrageous treatment where the treatment of foreign investment by the State itself is at issue;

- Since the 1920s, the substantive and procedural rights of the individual in international law have undergone considerable development. "To the modern eye, what is unfair or inequitable need not equate with the outrageous or the egregious";The minimum standard of treatment of aliens does not provide a tribunal with an "unfettered discretion to decide for itself, on a subjective basis, what was 'fair' or 'equitable' [...] without reference to established sources of law";

- "A State may treat foreign investment unfairly and inequitably without necessarily acting in bad faith";

- The vast number of IIAs adopting the FET standard forms a "body of concordant practice" that has influenced the content of the rules governing the treatment of foreign investment in current international law, going beyond the *Neer* standard (paras. 114–119).

ADF Group Inc v. United States, ICSID Case No ARB(AF)/00/1, Award, 9 January 2003

In this case the claimant, a Canadian steel supply company, challenged "Buy America" requirements that had forced it to source its processed steel inputs from United States companies. ADF claimed that the United States measures infringed NAFTA Article 1105, which, in the claimant's view, should be interpreted as eliminating barriers to trade in goods and services in order to attain the objectives of NAFTA. The tribunal held that Article 1105(1) had not been infringed as public procurement requirements of the type

/...

Box 13 (concluded)

used in this case were not so arbitrary or aberrant as to violate the customary international law standard. In the course of its decision, the tribunal cited and agreed with the above passages from the *Mondev* award (see para. 180) adding:

- [W]hat customary international law projects is not a static photograph of the minimum standard of treatment of aliens as it stood in 1927 when the Award in the Neer case was rendered. For both customary international law and the minimum standard of treatment of aliens it incorporates, are constantly in a process of development (para. 179);

- The *Neer* standard concerned protection against acts of private parties directed against the physical safety of foreigners while in the territory of a host State. The *Neer* formulation is not automatically extendible to the contemporary context of treatment of foreign investors and their investments by a host or recipient State;

- The investor has not shown that an autonomous requirement to accord fair and equitable treatment has been brought into the corpus of present day customary international law by the many hundreds of bilateral investment treaties;

- The *ADF* tribunal required the claimant to prove that an autonomous FET requirement has become a customary norm which, in that case, the claimant had failed to do so.

The tribunal in the *ADF* case was more cautious than the one in the *Mondev* case in its analysis of the extent to which the practice of States in concluding BITs can prove the existence of a general norm of international law in this field. Both awards affirmed, however, that the modern MST in not confined to the *Neer* standard, although neither of the two tribunals have offered a new legal test. An attempt to do so was undertaken in *Waste Management v. Mexico*, where the tribunal synthesized several earlier cases into the following paragraph:

> "*[T]he minimum standard of treatment of fair and equitable treatment is infringed by conduct attributable to the State and harmful to the claimant if the conduct is **arbitrary, grossly unfair, unjust or idiosyncratic, is discriminatory and exposes the claimant to sectional or racial prejudice, or involves a lack of due process leading to an outcome which offends judicial propriety** – as might be the case with a manifest failure of natural justice in judicial proceedings or a complete lack of transparency and candour in an administrative process. In applying this standard it is relevant that the treatment is in breach of representations made by the host State which were reasonably relied on by the claimant.*"[3]

In this case, the tribunal combined a number of earlier arbitral interpretations of the FET standard into its own understanding of the MST. The tribunal added that, "[e]vidently the standard is to some extent a flexible one which must be adapted to the circumstances of each case".[4]

The approach of the tribunal in *Waste Management* was followed in *GAMI v. Mexico* where the tribunal asserted that a number of implications arose out of the *Waste Management* analysis:

> "*Four implications of* Waste Management II *are salient... (1) The failure to fulfil the objectives of administrative regulations without more does not necessarily rise to a breach of international law. (2) A failure to satisfy requirements of national law does not necessarily violate international law. (3) Proof of a good faith effort by the Government to achieve the objectives of its laws and regulations may counter-balance instances of disregard of legal or regulatory requirements. (4)*

The record as a whole – not isolated events – determines *whether there has been a breach of international law.*"[5]

The tribunal in *Thunderbird v. Mexico* drew back from the standard as synthesized by the tribunal in *Waste Management* and returned to the explicit use of the MST as requiring a high threshold and thereby restricting the scope of the FET standard.[6] Here is the majority's interpretation of the scope of the MST under NAFTA Article 1105:

"194. The content of the minimum standard should not be rigidly interpreted and it should reflect evolving international customary law. Notwithstanding the evolution of customary law since decisions such as Neer *Claim in 1926, **the threshold for finding a violation of the minimum standard of treatment still remains high**, as illustrated by recent international jurisprudence. For the purposes of the present case, the Tribunal views acts that would give rise to a breach of the minimum standard of treatment prescribed by the NAFTA and customary international law as those that, weighed against the given factual context, amount to a **gross denial of justice or manifest arbitrariness falling below acceptable international standards**."* [Emphasis added]

On the facts, the tribunal found that the actions of the Mexican authorities did not come within that high threshold and the investor's claims were rejected. The high threshold for finding a violation ("the required severity of the conduct") was also emphasized in *Cargill v. Mexico*.[7]

The trend towards a more cautious interpretation of fair and equitable treatment under NAFTA Article 1105 is illustrated by the award in *Glamis Gold Ltd v. United States*[8] (box 14). The key element in the case as regards Article 1105 was the tribunal's acceptance of the United States Government's interpretation of the minimum standard of treatment of aliens which advocated the limited standard of review under the *Neer* doctrine and a high liability threshold. The tribunal accepted this with the understanding that the *Neer* standard could be adapted to modern considerations of egregious misconduct that might cover a wider range of actions than would be included under that standard in 1926. At the same time, the *Glamis* tribunal put an emphasis on the manner in which a rule of customary international law must be established.

Box 14. *Glamis Gold Ltd v. United States*, UNCITRAL Rules, Award, 8 June 2009

On the issue of fair and equitable treatment and the minimum standard of treatment the tribunal held:

600. The question thus becomes: what does this customary international law minimum standard of treatment require of a State Party vis-à-vis investors of another State Party? Is it the same as that established in 1926 in Neer v. Mexico?

601. As a threshold issue, the Tribunal notes that it is Claimant's burden to sufficiently answer each of these questions [...].

605. Claimant did provide numerous arbitral decisions in support of its conclusion that fair and equitable treatment encompasses a universe of "fundamental" principles common throughout the world that include "the duty to act in good faith, due process, transparency and candor, and fairness and protection from arbitrariness." Arbitral awards, Respondent rightly notes, do not constitute State practice and thus cannot create or prove customary international law. They can, however, serve as illustrations of customary international law if they involve an examination of customary international law, as opposed to a treaty-based, or autonomous, interpretation. [...]

611. The Tribunal [...] holds that it may look solely to arbitral awards – including BIT awards – that seek to be understood by

/...

Box 14 (continued)

reference to the customary international law minimum standard of treatment, as opposed to any autonomous standard. The Tribunal thus turns to its second task: determining the scope of the current customary international law minimum standard of treatment, as proven by Claimant.

612. It appears to this Tribunal that the NAFTA State Parties agree that, at a minimum, the fair and equitable treatment standard is that as articulated in Neer [...] Whether this standard has evolved since 1926, however, has not been definitively agreed upon. The Tribunal considers two possible types of evolution: (1) that what the international community views as "outrageous" may change over time; and (2) that the minimum standard of treatment has moved beyond what it was in 1926.

613. The Tribunal finds apparent agreement that the fair and equitable treatment standard is subject to the first type of evolution: a change in the international view of what is shocking and outrageous [...] this Tribunal holds that the Neer standard, when applied with current sentiments and to modern situations, may find shocking and egregious events not considered to reach this level in the past.

*614. **As regards the second form of evolution – the proposition that customary international law has moved beyond the minimum standard of treatment of aliens as defined in Neer – the Tribunal finds that the evidence provided by Claimant does not establish such evolution.** This is evident in the abundant and continued use of adjective modifiers throughout arbitral awards, evidencing a strict standard. International Thunderbird used the terms "gross denial of justice" and "manifest arbitrariness" to describe the acts that it viewed would breach the minimum standard of treatment. S.D.*

/...

Box 14 (continued)

Myers would find a breach of Article 1105 when an investor was treated "in such an unjust or arbitrary manner." The Mondev tribunal held: "The test is not whether a particular result is surprising, but whether the shock or surprise occasioned to an impartial tribunal leads, on reflection, to justified concerns as to the judicial propriety of the outcome. [...]

*615. **The customary international law minimum standard of treatment is just that, a minimum standard. It is meant to serve as a floor, an absolute bottom, below which conduct is not accepted by the international community.** Although the circumstances of the case are of course relevant, the standard is not meant to vary from state to state or investor to investor.* [...]

*616. It therefore appears that, **although situations may be more varied and complicated today than in the 1920s, the level of scrutiny is the same.** The fundamentals of the Neer standard thus still apply today: to violate the customary international law minimum standard of treatment codified in Article 1105 of the NAFTA, **an act must be sufficiently egregious and shocking – a gross denial of justice, manifest arbitrariness, blatant unfairness, a complete lack of due process, evident discrimination, or a manifest lack of reasons** – so as to fall below accepted international standards and constitute a breach of Article 1105(1). The Tribunal notes that one aspect of evolution from Neer that is generally agreed upon is that **bad faith is not required to find a violation of the fair and equitable treatment standard,** but its presence is conclusive evidence of such. Thus, an act that is egregious or shocking may also evidence bad faith, but such bad faith is not necessary for the finding of a violation. **The standard for finding a breach of the customary international law minimum standard of treatment therefore remains as stringent as it was***

/...

Box 14 (concluded)

under Neer; it is entirely possible, however that, as an international community, we may be shocked by State actions now that did not offend us previously. [...]

*627. [...] Such a breach may be exhibited by a "gross denial of justice or manifest arbitrariness falling below acceptable international standards;" **or the creation by the State of objective expectations in order to induce investment and the subsequent repudiation of those expectations.*** [Emphasis added, footnotes omitted]

The above review of different awards suggests, inter alia, that a simple illegality at the domestic level is insufficient to establish a breach of the standard; "something more" is required.[9] Indeed, claimants must satisfy a rather high evidential burden to show that the State conduct is notably arbitrary or grossly unfair and that the measure in question relates to an area effectively regulated by customary international law.[10]

However, the recent NAFTA award in *Merrill & Ring v. Canada*[11] goes in the opposite direction. In that case, the tribunal held that the stand-alone FET standard had become part of customary international law[12] and represents the latest stage in its evolution. It concluded:

"A requirement that aliens be treated fairly and equitably in relation to business, trade and investment [...] has become sufficiently part of widespread and consistent practice so as to demonstrate that it is reflected today in customary international law as opinio juris. *In the end, the name assigned to the standard does not really matter. What matters is that the standard protects against all such acts or behavior that might infringe a sense of fairness, equity and reasonableness. Of course, the concepts of fairness, equitableness and reasonableness cannot be defined precisely: they require to be*

applied to the facts of each case. In fact, the concept of fair and equitable treatment has emerged to make possible the consideration of inappropriate behavior of a sort, which while difficult to define, may still be regarded as unfair, inequitable or unreasonable." (para. 210).

Accordingly, the standard went far beyond the limited elements of the *Neer* case. Indeed, the tribunal found that "this standard provides for the fair and equitable treatment of alien investors within the confines of reasonableness".[13] This appears, at first glance, to reaffirm a very expansive reading of the FET standard, while at the same time saying that this actually represents the customary minimum standard. The *Merrill & Ring* tribunal failed to give cogent reasons for its conclusion that the MST made such a leap in its evolution, and by doing so has deprived the 2001 NAFTA Interpretative Statement of any practical effect. This award added to the confusion as to the appropriate approach under NAFTA.

As a result of arbitral practice under NAFTA to date, three approaches can be identified as regards the content of the minimum standard of treatment of aliens and its relationship with fair and equitable treatment:

(a) MST is equated to the standard of treatment set by the *Neer* case in terms of the level of scrutiny (high liability threshold), although that standard has evolved in terms of what may be seen as "shocking" or "egregious" today. The standard has been set out as requiring "a gross denial of justice, manifest arbitrariness, blatant unfairness, a complete lack of due process, evident discrimination, or a manifest lack of reasons" (*Glamis v. United States*);[14]

(b) MST goes beyond the *Neer* standard, as the latter was formulated to address a narrow and particular group of situations. The liability threshold is not as high as under the first approach. One tribunal attempted to synthesize the standard by referring to conduct that is "arbitrary, grossly unfair, unjust or idiosyncratic" or that is "discriminatory and exposes the claimant to sectional or racial prejudice", or which involves a "complete lack of transparency and candour in an administrative process" (*Waste Management v. Mexico*);

(c) MST in its modern state is no different from an obligation to provide fair and equitable treatment when the latter is interpreted literally (low liability threshold). As such, it is said to protect "against all such acts or behaviour that might infringe a sense of fairness, equity and reasonableness" (*Merrill & Ring v. Canada*).[15]

The existence of different approaches per se makes it difficult to predict which one will be adopted by a tribunal in a particular case. The one point common to all three approaches is that there is no need for proof of bad faith on the part of the host country authorities, although such proof would be conclusive that a breach had occurred.

In discussing the content of the MST, it should be recalled that it is part of customary international law that applies in inter-State relations, regardless of whether there exists a treaty between the States concerned. A tribunal giving a particular interpretation of the MST is interpreting a general customary international obligation that applies in relations between all States. The repercussions of particular interpretation go beyond the relationship between the contracting parties to the applicable IIA; they extend to the international community as a whole. This emphasizes the high responsibility of arbitrators interpreting the standard.

3. Awards applying other types of FET clauses

A number of arbitral tribunals have dealt with the two types of FET clauses that are not expressly linked to the minimum standard of treatment of aliens: (a) an unqualified FET clause; and (b) FET clauses linked to international law (see sections II.C and II.D). There has been no consistent approach to deciding whether the content of those clauses should be derived from the MST. Some tribunals have found that such clauses can be equated with the MST.[16] Others, on the contrary, have ignored a reference to international law in the clause and adopted the "plain meaning" interpretation as if it were an unqualified FET clause.[17] Still other panels chose not to address the issue at all.[18]

Several tribunals have held that the actual content of the unqualified FET standard is not materially different from the MST.[19] A number of tribunals, while opting for an autonomous interpretation, have quoted and relied upon the legal tests elaborated in the NAFTA cases interpreting the minimum standard of treatment under Article 1105.[20] One tribunal said that the threshold for finding a violation of an unqualified FET obligation was still a *"high one"*;[21] another tribunal suggested that *"in order to violate the [unqualified FET] standard, it may be sufficient that States' conduct displays a **relatively lower degree of inappropriateness**"*, compared with the MST.[22] In short, arbitral tribunals have displayed some confusion on how particular types of FET clauses relate to the international minimum standard.

4. Is convergence on the content of FET in sight?

The differences in existing approaches make it hard to arrive at a settled view of the relationship between FET and the MST. At the same time, there are signs of an emerging trend of convergence of FET obligations, no matter how they are expressed, into a number of common requirements for State conduct. Indeed, in a number of recent cases, arbitrators seemed to be less interested in the theoretical discussion on the relationship between the FET and the MST and turned their attention primarily to the content of the FET obligation, whether or not it is qualified by the MST. In other words, more attention is being paid to singling and fleshing out specific requirements within the broad FET standard with a view to establishing its more distinct and detailed content. Schill has summarized the reasons that have contributed to this convergence in the following terms:

> *"First, some tribunals consider that the inclusion of the FET in the vast web of investment treaties has transformed the standard itself into customary international law. Secondly, even in the absence of such an explicit transformation, other tribunals interpret the international minimum standard as an evolutionary concept that has developed since the days of traditional international law, thus levelling possible differences between treaty and custom. [...] Finally, the customary international law minimum standard itself lacks precise content and is in need of interpretation by arbitral tribunals. In order to concretize such a standard, arbitral tribunals generally recur to the decisions of other arbitral tribunals without distinguishing whether those decisions were based on the customary variant or an autonomous treaty standard."* (Schill, 2010, p. 153)

The elements forming this emerging shared substantive content of the FET standard are considered in the next section.

Importantly, however, despite the shared content, the minimum standard of treatment of aliens is still typically understood and interpreted as a more demanding standard, in terms of the liability threshold, than an unqualified FET obligation. As shown in box 15, statistically there is a significant difference between the claimants' rate of success under the two contrasting types of FET clauses. Statistics suggest that it is more difficult for a claimant to establish a violation of FET under NAFTA than under a BIT. In cases under NAFTA (which links the FET standard to MST), the claimants' success rate is much lower than in cases under traditional BITs, where the FET provision is most often analysed as setting an autonomous standard not linked to the MST.

Box 15. Statistics on FET claims

By October 2010, tribunals addressed the merits of FET claims in 84 treaty-based disputes.[a] Of this overall number, the FET claim was accepted in 45 cases and rejected in 39 cases.

There is a significant statistical difference between NAFTA disputes and BIT disputes.[b] In NAFTA cases, only 22 per cent of those claims were accepted (4 out of 18); in BIT cases, 62 per cent were accepted (41 out of 66).

Source: UNCTAD

Notes:

[a] This number excludes cases dismissed on jurisdictional grounds as well as rulings where the merits of the FET claim were not addressed due to a finding of expropriation. Only public awards have been counted.

[b] For statistical purposes, this group includes disputes brought under the Energy Charter Treaty.

B. Emerging substantive content of the FET standard

As mentioned in the previous section, tribunals have been increasingly moving away from the discussion of the relationship between the FET standard and the minimum standard of treatment of aliens. Instead, they have focused their efforts on discerning the substantive content of the standard, i.e. identifying the specific elements that the standard consists of, taking into account the myriad of different specific factual contexts.

Many arbitral tribunals have pointed out that the FET standard does not imply adjudication ex aqueo et bono, but represents a rule of law with specific content.[23] Fleshing out the elements of this content is an ongoing process, in which tribunals play a critical role. One arbitrator has even suggested that the term "fair and equitable treatment" is "an intentionally vague term, designed to give adjudicators a quasi-legislative authority to articulate a variety of rules necessary to achieve the treaty's object and purpose in particular disputes" (Brower II, 2003, p. 66). It is true that investment tribunals have largely been responsible for developing the content of the standard.

> "*As a matter of orthodoxy, States create international law, while international courts merely interpret and apply it.* [...] *In practice, however, international courts play a critical role in the development of international law because the distinction between interpreting and creating the law is a fiction.* [...] [Courts are required] *to interpret broad provisions, fill gaps, and clarify ambiguities. These judicial interpretations are then routinely* looked to – by states, *other courts, and academics – as evidence of the content of international law*" (Roberts, 2010, p. 188).

At this point of the development of the FET obligation, it is possible to single out certain types of improper and discreditable State conduct that would constitute a violation of the standard. Such relevant concepts include:

(a) Defeating investors' legitimate expectations (in balance with the host State's right to regulate in public interest);

(b) Denial of justice and due process;

(c) Manifest arbitrariness in decision-making;

(d) Discrimination;

(e) Outright abusive treatment.

The following sections will briefly review the mentioned elements of the FET standard, recognizing that its application is intricately tied to the facts of the specific cases, and therefore, the abstract criteria can provide only rough guidelines. Additionally, this section addresses the role of investor conduct and the question of the appropriate threshold for finding a State responsible.

A number of possible elements, such as transparency or consistency, have generated concern and criticism. So far, they may not be said to have materialized into the content of fair and equitable treatment with a sufficient degree of support.[24]

FET clauses typically refer to "treatment" of investments. "Treatment" is an expansive term, defined as "[c]onduct, behaviour; action or behaviour towards a person".[25] Essentially, any action or omission attributable to the host State can become a subject of an FET claim.[26] While historic cases on the international minimum standard and denial of justice were typically concerned with alleged failures in the judicial system of the host State, modern FET claims cover, in addition, all types of administrative and legislative decisions, as well as the conduct of any body or entity if this conduct is attributable to the State.

1. Legitimate expectations

Protection of investors' legitimate expectations has been repeatedly identified by arbitral tribunals as a key element of the FET standard.[27] The concept of legitimate expectations is connected to the phenomenon of "change". Investments are not one-off transactions; they typically involve economic projects of significant duration, such as business concessions, and many do not have any time limitation at all, for example, foreign-owned manufacturing enterprises and service providers. With the long duration of a project there comes a risk that the conditions of the investment's operation will change, producing a negative impact on the investment concerned.

There can be different reasons behind changes to the business environment: Some are due to purely economic factors, such as technological innovations, the rising and falling of prices and the relative economic power of competitors. Others arise from the conduct of the host State government, specific or general measures, action or inaction. It is with the latter that the FET standard is concerned. As all businesses, foreign investments are subject to governmental regulation. Sometimes, especially with respect to large-scale business projects, there is a direct contractual relationship between the investor and a host State government, which provides scope for a governmental interference with contractual rights. It not uncommon that changes of host country policies follow changes in the political landscape within the State.

Claims relating to breach of legitimate expectations arise in situations when an investor is suffering losses due to the changes brought about by certain State measures. In other words, when a host State's conduct causes adverse effects to an investment, that is, it reduces its economic value, an investor may allege that the State violates legitimate expectations that the investor had when making the investment. The question is thus whether, and to what degree, the FET standard includes protection of such legitimate expectations. A particularly important subquestion concerns the kind of expectations that can be considered legitimate.

The concept of legitimate expectations has been used in arbitral decisions applying all types of FET clauses. It has been applied either on its own or in tandem with other related concepts such as "regulatory stability". Some awards have adopted a so-called "pro-investor" approach, essentially reading into the FET standard the obligation to maintain a stable legal and business framework.[28] Other cases have established that legitimate expectations may only be created where a number of qualifying requirements are present.

Focus on the stable legal and business framework. The classic statement of the permissive position is found in the tribunal's award in *Tecmed v. Mexico* (box 16). This approach would require that the host country authorities act consistently, without ambiguity and transparently, making sure the investor knows in advance the regulatory and administrative policies and practices to which it will be subject, so that it may comply. The list is indeed demanding and nearly impossible to achieve. As Douglas has noted, "[t]he Tecmed 'standard' is actually not a standard at all; it is rather a description of perfect public regulation in a perfect world, to which all states should aspire but very few (if any) will ever attain" (Douglas, 2006, p. 28).

Box 16. *Tecmed v. Mexico*, ICSID Case No ARB (AF)/00/2, Award, 29 May 2003

This dispute concerned the replacement of an open licence for the operation of a landfill site by a licence of limited duration. The claimant alleged that this change in the legal and business environment of the investment amounted to a breach of the FET standard in Article 4(1) of the BIT between Spain and Mexico which states:

"Each Contracting Party shall guarantee fair and equitable treatment in its territory pursuant to international law for investments made • by investors from another Contracting Party [...]"

The tribunal upheld this claim on the grounds that the Mexican authorities had acted in an ambiguous and uncertain way in their actions regarding the replacement of the licence, thereby infringing the legitimate expectations of the claimant.

The tribunal set out the general principle to be applied in para.154:

"The Arbitral Tribunal considers that this provision of the Agreement, in light of the good faith principle established by international law, requires the Contracting Parties to provide to international investments treatment that does not affect the basic

/...

Box 16 (concluded)

expectations that were taken into account by the foreign investor to make the investment. The foreign investor expects the host State to act in a consistent manner, free from ambiguity and totally transparently in its relations with the foreign investor, so that it may know beforehand any and all rules and regulations that will govern its investments, as well as the goals of the relevant policies and administrative practices or directives, to be able to plan its investment and comply with such regulations."

Some cases have followed this approach. Thus in *CMS v. Argentina* and *Enron v. Argentina*, the tribunals felt that the FET standard included the requirement of a "stable framework for the investment". In reaching this conclusion, both tribunals relied on the preamble of the applicable Argentina-United States BIT, which said explicitly that "fair and equitable treatment of investment is desirable in order to maintain a stable framework for investment".[29] On the facts, the tribunal held that the emergency measures taken by Argentina in the wake of the Peso crisis of 2000–2002 were in breach of the FET standard, as they had dismantled the regime of tariff guarantees that had originally induced the investor to invest, thereby undermining any stable framework for investment.[30] Notably, the tribunal dismissed the reasons for Argentina's conduct as irrelevant to the determination of whether a breach has occurred: "Even assuming that the Respondent was guided by the best of intentions, which the Tribunal has no reasons to doubt, there is here an objective breach [of the FET standard]".[31]

Similarly, in *PSEG v. Turkey*, the tribunal emphasized that the changes in both the legislative environment as well as in the attitudes and policies of the administration relating to investments were contrary to the need to "ensure a stable and predictable business environment for investors to operate in, as required [...] by the Treaty".[32] The situation in that case was complicated by the fact that the laws had been changed continuously, thereby creating a "roller-coaster" effect for the investor and undermining the predictability of the legal regime.

In *Occidental v. Ecuador*, the tribunal equated the requirement of a stable and predictable legal and business framework for investment with the international law standard.[33] It then concluded that Ecuador's changes to its tax regime for oil export had changed the underlying legal and business framework for the investment and amounted to a breach of the FET standard.[34]

In these cases, tribunals have gone so far as to suggest that any adverse change in the business or legal framework of the host country may give rise to a breach of the FET standard in that the investors' legitimate expectations of predictability and stability are thereby undermined. This approach is unjustified, as it would potentially prevent the host State from introducing any legitimate regulatory change, let alone from undertaking a regulatory reform that may be called for. It ignores the fact that investors should legitimately expect regulations to change over time as an aspect of the normal operation of legal and policy processes of the economy they operate in. Considerations of this kind have led some tribunals to require further qualifying elements to the notion of investors' legitimate expectations.

Legitimate expectations subject to qualifying requirements. In order to avoid an overbroad reading of the FET standard by reference to legitimate expectations, several awards have sought to identify factors that delimit the scope of such expectations. This appears to be a more sensible approach, as an investor's legitimate expectations must be grounded in reality, experience and context. In *Duke Energy v. Ecuador*, the tribunal stressed the need to consider all the circumstances:

> *"The stability of the legal and business environment is directly linked to the investor's justified expectations. The Tribunal acknowledges that such expectations are an important element*

*of fair and equitable treatment. At the same time, it is mindful of their limitations. To be protected, the investor's expectations must be **legitimate and reasonable** at the time when the investor makes the investment. The assessment of the reasonableness or legitimacy must take into account all circumstances, including not only the facts surrounding the investment, but also the **political, socioeconomic, cultural and historical conditions prevailing in the host State**. In addition, such expectations **must arise from the conditions that the State offered the investor and the latter must have relied upon them when deciding to invest**.*"[35] [Emphasis added]

This statement allows for a contextualization of what an investor can legitimately expect from the host country authorities. It also requires looking closely at the causal link between the investment and a specific promise made by the State to the investor.

From the statement of tribunals in *Duke Energy v. Ecuador* and other cases,[36] it is possible to identify a number of key qualifying elements:

(a) Legitimate expectations may arise only from a State's specific representations or commitments made to the investor, on which the latter has relied;

(b) The investor must be aware of the general regulatory environment in the host country;

(c) Investors' expectations must be balanced against legitimate regulatory activities of host countries.

Specific representations. The need for specific representations was stressed in *Methanex v. United States*, a NAFTA dispute.[37] There the claimant, a Canadian producer of methanol, challenged Californian legislation that banned the production of gasoline containing methanol-based additives on environmental grounds. The investor claimed a violation, inter alia, of NAFTA's FET obligation, arguing that the ban was unjustified, destroyed its market and discriminated in favour of the United States domestic ethanol industry. In rejecting this claim, the tribunal attached particular importance to the fact that *Methanex* had not been given any representations by the United States that it could reasonably have relied upon to conclude that such regulatory changes would not occur.[38]

Arbitral decisions suggest in this regard that an investor may derive legitimate expectations either from (a) specific commitments addressed to it personally, for example, in the form of a stabilization clause,[39] or (b) rules that are not specifically addressed to a particular investor but which are put in place with a specific aim to induce foreign investments and on which the foreign investor relied in making his investment.[40] In *Enron v. Argentina* and *LG&E v. Argentina*, no particular undertakings were made to the claimants. However, the guarantees included in the domestic legislation were found to constitute a promise to foreign investors as a class and were deemed sufficient to create legitimate expectations.[41] Conversely, in *Metalpar v. Argentina*, the tribunal found that there had been no "licence, permit or contract of any kind" between Argentina and the claimants and that therefore the claimants had no grounds for legitimate expectations.[42]

Where a government extends these types of commitments to investors, this significantly curbs and restricts its powers to change the rules of the game in the future. As noted by the tribunal in *CMS v. Argentina*:

> "*It is not a question of whether the legal framework might need to be frozen as it can always evolve and be adapted to changing circumstances, but neither is it a question of whether the framework can be dispensed with altogether when specific commitments to the contrary have been made. The law of foreign investment and its protection has been developed with*

the specific objective of avoiding such adverse legal effects."[43]
[Emphasis added]

The tribunal established in that case that the general guarantees given by Argentina under the domestic legal framework were "crucial for the investment decision".[44] This is in line with other cases which have also held that representations must have been relied upon by the investor when deciding to invest.[45]

In some cases involving a contractual relationship between an investor and a host State, a claimant put forward an argument that it had a legitimate expectation to have its contract performed by the State and that, therefore, any violation of the contract by the State amounted to a violation of the FET obligation. Tribunals have disagreed and distinguished legitimate expectations under international law from contractual rights. In *Parkerings v. Lithuania*, the tribunal stated that "[N]ot every hope amounts to an expectation under international law [...] [C]ontracts involve intrinsic expectations from each party that do not amount to expectations as understood in international law".[46]

Similarly, the tribunal in *Hamester v. Ghana* concluded that "it is not sufficient for a claimant to invoke contractual rights that have allegedly been infringed to sustain a claim for a violation of the FET standard".[47] The opposite approach would put all investor-State contracts under the protection of the FET standard, and the latter would effectively constitute a broadly interpreted umbrella clause. (Schreuer, 2007, p. 18.)

Arbitral tribunals have also held that investors carry an obligation to perform their due diligence and not to rely solely on representations and assurances of the host government. In *MTD v. Chile*; the Malaysian claimant, a property development company specialized in urban development, successfully argued that the FET standard had been breached by Chile when its Foreign Investment Commission had authorized a major property development investment by the claimant in violation of existing Chilean planning regulations. Granting an investment authorization by the body of the host State, despite the fact that it was contrary to the laws of the host State itself, gave rise to legitimate expectations. However the amount of damages awarded was reduced by 50 per cent on the basis that the investor should have made an independent assessment of its legal situation.[48]

The moment when a representation is made can be of importance. A number of tribunals have held that the expectations to be taken into account are those existing at the time when the investor made the decision to invest.[49] Depending on the context, however, specific assurances can give rise to legitimate expectations even where these assurances are given after the investment has been made.[50]

Presumption of awareness of general regulatory environment. In *Methanex v. United States*, discussed above, the tribunal stressed the need for the investor to have a general awareness of the regulatory environment in which it was operating as a condition for the application of the legitimate expectations doctrine. As already mentioned above, Methanex had entered into a political economy:

> "... in which it was widely known, if not notorious, that governmental environmental and health protection institutions at the federal and state level [...] continuously monitored the use and impact of chemical compounds and commonly prohibited or restricted the use of some of those compounds for environmental and/or health reasons."[51]

Investors should also be aware and take into account the level of the country's development and administrative practices. Indeed, investors are often attracted to developing countries by the possibility of earning a higher rate of return on their capital compared to investment opportunities in more developed economies. It is normal that the prospects of greater profits are accompanied by greater risks, including in the regulatory sphere.[52]

In *Genin v. Estonia*, the tribunal found that there was no breach of FET taking into account the fact that the claimants had knowingly chose to invest in:

> "... *a renascent independent state, coming rapidly to grips with the reality of modern financial, commercial and banking practices and the emergence of state institutions responsible for overseeing and regulating areas of activity perhaps previously unknown.*"[53]

Likewise, in *Parkerings-Compagniet v. Lithuania*, the tribunal noted that Lithuania was a country in political transition and therefore, the investor should have regarded changes in the legislative regime as likely. In such a situation, no expectation that the laws would remain unchanged could be legitimate. An investor faced with this situation accepts the business risk of instability and should protect its legitimate expectations by introducing a contractual clause that protects against unexpected legal changes.[54]

Several tribunals have considered transparency and participation as part of an investor's legitimate expectations.[55] Transparency is not an end in itself; it is a means to achieve better governance and avoid arbitrary and discriminatory conduct. While there is no doubt that transparency in the conduct towards, and consultation with, the investor is a good practice, not all countries have the regulatory and institutional framework in place to allow for full transparency and participation. Very few countries can claim to be fully transparent in their regulatory decision-making and implementation process. An inflexible and unrealistic approach to these issues would in effect transfer the risk of operating in a developing country environment from an investor to the host State.

Balancing investors' expectations against legitimate regulatory action. A significant number of awards have emphasized the need to balance investor expectations against the legitimate regulatory goals of the host country. They suggest that the FET obligation does not prevent host States from acting in public interest even if such acts adversely affect investments. This is an important qualification to the legitimate expectations approach.

The foundations for this approach were laid in *Saluka v. Czech Republic.*[56] In the course of this decision the tribunal analysed the balancing process involved in a claim based on breach of legitimate expectations:

> "[Legitimate] *expectations, in order for them to be protected, must rise to the level of legitimacy and reasonableness in light of the circumstances. [...] No investor may reasonably expect that the circumstances prevailing at the time the investment is made remain totally unchanged. In order to determine whether frustration of the foreign investor's expectations was justified and reasonable,* **the host State's legitimate right subsequently to regulate domestic matters in the public interest must be taken into consideration as well.** *[...] The determination of a breach of Article 3.1 by the Czech Republic therefore requires a* **weighing of the Claimant's legitimate and reasonable expectations on the one hand and the Respondent's legitimate regulatory interests on the other.***[...]*
>
> *A foreign investor [...] may in any case properly expect that the Czech Republic implements its policies* bona fide *by conduct that is, as far as it affects the investors' investment, reasonably justifiable by public policies and that such conduct does not* **manifestly violate the requirements of consistency, transparency, even-handedness and nondiscrimination.** *[...]*
>
> *[T]he host State must never disregard the principles of procedural propriety and due process and must grant the investor freedom from coercion or harassment by its own regulatory authorities."*[57] [Emphasis added]

The tribunal thus recognized the host State's right to enact public-interest legislation, even if the changes negatively affect a foreign investor.[58] Such conduct will not be considered as defeating the investors' legitimate expectations and violating the FET standard, as long it is implemented by the government in a bona fide manner. Recent arbitral awards have emphasized that this holds true where no specific guarantees were given to the investor regarding the stability of the regulatory environment.

The interpretation of the FET obligation as permitting public-interest regulation has also appeared in more recent cases.

Thus, in *Parkerings-Compagniet v. Lithuania*, the tribunal held that each State had an undeniable right to exercise its sovereign legislative power – albeit in a reasonable and fair manner – and that an investor must anticipate a possible change of circumstances, and thus structure its investment in order to adapt it to the new legal environment, particularly of a country in transition. The tribunal rejected the FET claim, concluding that the Republic of Lithuania had not given any explicit or implicit promise that the legal framework of the investment would remain unchanged.[59] The award stated in particular:

> "*It is each State's undeniable right and privilege to exercise its sovereign legislative power. A State has the right to enact, modify or cancel a law at its own discretion. Save for the existence of an agreement, in the form of a stabilisation clause or otherwise, there is nothing objectionable about the amendment brought to the regulatory framework existing at the time an investor made its investment. As a matter of fact, any businessman or investor knows that laws will evolve over time. What is prohibited however is for a State to act unfairly, unreasonably or inequitably in the exercise of its legislative power.*"[60]

In *Continental Casualty v. Argentina*, the tribunal specifically noted that stability of the legal framework for investments, mentioned in the preamble of the applicable BIT, was not a legal obligation in itself for the Contracting Parties and that "it would be unconscionable for a country to promise not to change its legislation as time and needs change".[61] In the view of the tribunal, "[s]uch an implication as to stability in the BIT's Preamble would be contrary to an effective interpretation of the Treaty; reliance on such an implication by a foreign investor would be misplaced and, indeed, unreasonable."[62]

In *Vivendi v. Argentina II*, the tribunal accepted that a newly elected government with a policy perspective different from its predecessor was entitled to reverse course. However, the tribunal suggested that this change should be accompanied by a transparent and non-coercive renegotiation of the contract at issue, and not through threats of rescission based on colourable allegations of impropriety.[63]

In *EDF v. Romania*,[64] the claimant invested in two joint-venture companies with Romanian government agencies to provide airport services, including duty-free services, at Bucharest Airport and with the national airline of Romania TAROM. The grounds of claim were that the claimant had built up a successful duty-free business and that, following a change of government, it had been unfairly deprived of that business. The claimant alleged that it had been so treated as it had refused to pay a bribe to officials involved in the renewal of the joint-venture agreements. In particular, the claimant alleged that it had a legitimate expectation that its continued involvement in the business was assured, based on the terms of the contracts and on the conduct of Romanian officials, and that failure to meet this expectation constituted a breach of the FET standard.

The tribunal noted the following:

"The idea that legitimate expectations, and therefore FET, im*ply the stability of the legal and business framework, may not be correct if stated in an overly-broad and unqualified formulation. The FET might then mean the virtual freezing of the legal regulation of economic activities, in contrast with the State's normal regulatory power and the evolutionary character of economic life.* **Except where specific promises or representations are made by the State to the investor, the latter may not rely on a bilateral investment treaty as a kind of insurance policy against the risk of any changes in the host State's legal and economic framework. Such expectation would be neither legitimate nor reasonable.**"[65] [Emphasis added]

Echoing the tribunal's view in *Saluka v. Czech Republic*, the tribunal in *EDF v. Romania* added:

"Legitimate expectations cannot be solely the subjective expectations of the investor. They must be examined as the expectations at the time the investment is made, as they may be deduced from all the circumstances of the case, **due regard being paid to the host State's power to regulate its economic life in the public interest.**"[66] [Emphasis added]

In this case, there was no evidence of bribe solicitation by the governmental officials. However, the tribunal mentioned that had such evidence been present, the relevant conduct would amount to a breach of the FET standard.[67] Equally, the claimant could not show that it had legitimate grounds to expect continued involvement in the business or that the Romanian authorities' actions in terminating that involvement had infringed applicable rules of Romanian law.[68] A statute passed to abolish duty-free operations in Romanian airports was held to be a proportionate response to the incidence of contraband activities being carried out at such operations and did not impact disproportionately, or in a discriminatory manner, on the claimant's investments as only one of its duty-free outlets was affected and the statute applied equally to all other duty-free operators at Romanian airports.[69]

Conclusions. The reference by arbitral tribunals to legitimate expectations to find a violation of fair and equitable treatment cannot be applied in isolation from the actual regulatory, economic, social and political context and without consideration of the balancing required between investor expectations and the function of States as guardians of the public interest, exercised through their right to regulate. This is particularly important in developing countries. The concept of equity and equitable treatment will need to take into account, not only the interests of investors, but those of the host State as well, calling for an appropriate balance between various legitimate interests involved. The appropriateness of the proportionality principle and balancing through partial compensation could be explored as possible tools to help in this process.

There are certain limitations as to what expectations can be considered legitimate and protected by the FET standard. In particular, investors must anticipate and accept that the regulatory and legislative environment may change over time. In light of the FET standard, investors can expect, however, that such changes will be implemented in good faith and in a non-abusive manner and that public-interest arguments will not be used as a disguise for arbitrary and discriminatory measures. The power of States to regulate without compensating foreign investors will also be limited where it makes specific assurances to the investor about keeping in place certain aspects of the business or legal regime. Similarly, general regulations that are put in place specifically to induce foreign investments and on which an investor relies can expose a State to liability if it subsequently decides to change or withdraw those regulations. Liability may be avoided if the treaty includes general exceptions that may justify the relevant State conduct (see section IV, policy option 6).

Investors have a due diligence obligation to determine the extent of the risk to which they are subjected, including country and regulatory risks, and to have expectations that are reasonable in all the circumstances. In particular, when planning their investments, investors should take account of the conditions in the particular host State, including the standards of governance and regulatory development prevailing in that State.

2. Manifest arbitrariness

Existing arbitral awards have mostly analysed arbitrariness in the context of a separate BIT obligation that prohibits arbitrary measures. However, several tribunals have emphasized that prohibition of arbitrariness is part and parcel of the FET standard. In its ordinary meaning, "arbitrary" means "derived from mere opinion", "capricious", "unrestrained", "despotic".[70] Arbitral conduct has been described as "founded on prejudice or preference rather than on reason or fact".[71] Arbitrariness in decision-making has to do with the motivations and objectives behind the conduct concerned. A measure that inflicts damage on the investor without serving any legitimate purpose and without a rational explanation, but that instead rests on prejudice or bias, would be considered arbitrary.[72]

In the *ELSI* case, the International Court of Justice stated that an act illegal under domestic law is not necessarily arbitrary under international law.[73] That ruling suggests a deferential standard of review. Establishing some rational relationship to the alleged objective of a measure should be sufficient for a measure to be considered non-arbitrary, even if it is unwise, inefficient or not the best course of action in the circumstances. Thus, in *Enron v. Argentina*, when analyzing Argentina's measures taken in the context of the 2000–2002 financial crisis, the tribunal held:

> *"The measures adopted might have been **good or bad, a matter which is not for the Tribunal to judge**, and as concluded they*

were not consistent with the domestic and the Treaty legal framework, but **they were not arbitrary in that they were what the Government believed and understood was the best response to the unfolding crisis.** *Irrespective of the question of intention, a finding of arbitrariness requires that* **some important measure of impropriety** *is manifest, and this is not found in a process which although far from desirable is nonetheless not entirely surprising in the context it took place.*"[74] [Emphasis added]

In a similar vein, the tribunal in *LG&E v. Argentina*, a case arising from the same crisis, held that "[e]ven though the measures adopted by Argentina may not have been the best, **they were not taken lightly, without due consideration**".[75] [Emphasis added]

The range of legitimate policies is potentially very broad and not limited to oft-mentioned goals of environmental protection, public heath or consumer protection. For example, one recent decision held that an introduction of administrative pricing on energy was motivated by the State's desire to reduce excessive profits earned by the generators (investors). The tribunal found that this was "a perfectly valid and rational policy objective for a government to address luxury profits".[76]

Another facet of arbitrariness is that it refers to a conduct that constitutes a wilful disregard of due process of law.[77] For example, a blatant disregard of applicable tender rules, distorting fair competition among tender participants, was held to be arbitrary.[78] The violation must indeed be blatant or manifest (see section III.B.7).

Notably, in *Enron, LG&E* and a number of other cases, the State conduct at issue was found to be violating the FET standard, but at the same time, not arbitrary. This demonstrates that the criterion of arbitrariness is narrower than the FET obligation. It is also clear that the prohibition of arbitrary conduct does not prevent States from regulating in public interest.

3. Denial of justice and due process

Compliance with the most basic due process requirements is necessary to avoid a denial of justice.

Denial of justice is traditionally defined as any gross misadministration of justice by domestic courts resulting from the ill-functioning of the State's judicial system (Focarelli, 2009). It is generally recognized that only gross or manifest instances of injustice are considered a denial of justice and that a simple error, misinterpretation or misapplication of domestic law is not per se a denial of justice.[79] While it is commonly emphasized that any attempt accurately and exhaustively to define the forms of denial of justice is bound to fail, the following are likely to be considered a denial of justice:[80]

(a) Denial of access to justice and the refusal of courts to decide;

(b) Unreasonable delay in proceedings;

(c) Lack of a court's independence from the legislative and the executive branches of the State;[81]

(d) Failure to execute final judgments or arbitral awards;

(e) Corruption of a judge;

(f) Discrimination against the foreign litigant;[82]

(g) Breach of fundamental due process guarantees, such as a failure to give notice of the proceedings and failure to provide an opportunity to be heard.

An important element of the denial-of-justice delict is the requirement to exhaust local remedies. This is based on the rationale that the delict is concerned with the system of national justice (not a single court or judge); when local remedies are still effectively available the judicial ill-treatment may still be corrected by higher courts.[83] It is well established that "an aberrant decision by an official lower in the hierarchy, which is capable of being reconsidered, does not of itself amount to an unlawful act [under international law]".[84]

The length of the delay required in order for a denial of justice to arise is unclear. It was held in *Jan de Nul v. Egypt* that the period of 10 years to obtain a first instance judgement was "certainly unsatisfactory", but did not rise to the level of a denial of justice because "the issues were complex and highly technical, that two cases were involved, that the parties were especially productive in terms of submissions and filed extensive expert reports".[85]

While the classic concept of denial of justice is confined to courts, some investment treaties refer to all types of "legal or administrative proceedings".[86] Indeed, the majority of modern-day FET claims relate to measures taken by the executive, and sometimes legislative, branches of a government.[87] The fundamental requirements of due process are applicable there, too. As previously noted, States retain the right to regulate in the public interest but they must do so without violating the due process of law. The latter effectively requires governments to implement their decisions in a non-abusive manner (see section III.B.5). Procedural deficiencies of non-fundamental and non-abusive nature can contribute to a finding a violation,[88] but they will not be sufficient for establishing a breach, if the measure itself is legitimate.[89]

4. Discrimination

Tribunals have held that the FET standard prohibits discriminatory treatment of foreign investors and their investments.[90] The non-discrimination standard that forms part of the FET standard should not be confused with the treaty obligation to grant the most favourable treatment to the investor and its investment (UNCTAD, 2010a, pp.15–16). While the national treatment and MFN standards deal with nationality-based discrimination, the non-discrimination requirement as part of the FET standard appears to prohibit discrimination in the sense of specific targeting of a foreign investor on other manifestly wrongful grounds such as gender, race or religious belief, or the types of conduct that amount to a "deliberate conspiracy […] to destroy or frustrate the investment".[91] A measure is likely to be found to violate the FET standard if it evidently singles out (de jure or de facto) the claimant and there is no legitimate justification for the measure.

There are, however, divergent views on the role of non-discrimination, as was found by the tribunal in *Grand River Enterprises v. United States*. The tribunal held that "neither Article 1105 nor the customary international law standard of protection generally prohibits discrimination against foreign investments".[92]

5. Abusive treatment

Abusive conduct includes coercion, duress and harassment that involve unwarranted and improper pressure, abuse of power, persecution, threats, intimidation and use of force. Abusive conduct can potentially take many forms, such as arresting or jailing of executives or personnel; threats of or initiation of criminal proceedings; deliberate imposition of unfounded tax assessments, criminal or other fines; arresting or seizing of physical assets, bank accounts and equity; interfering with, obstructing or preventing daily business operations; and deportation from the host State or refusal to extend documents that allow a foreigner to live and work in the host State.

Clearly, there are situations where the enumerated actions will be justified and proper under the host State law; the conduct of the State will be abusive where there are manifestly no lawful grounds for the relevant actions and the harm is inflicted upon the investment for improper reasons, such as national prejudice or political revenge. The chances of finding an FET breach on account of abusive treatment are especially high if episodes of harassment and coercion are "repeated and sustained",[93] amount to a "deliberate conspiracy [...] to destroy or frustrate the investment"[94] or a "conspiracy to take away legitimately acquired rights".[95]

The tribunal in *Saluka* held that fair and equitable treatment requires the host State to "grant the investor freedom from coercion or harassment by its own regulatory authorities".[96] In *Desert Line Projects*, the tribunal found that the claimant had suffered "threats and attacks" attributable to the respondent State, including arrests of the claimant's employees and family members and armed interference with the claimant's equipment. The tribunal further found that the Settlement Agreement, the terms of which had been extremely unfavourable for the investor, had been "imposed onto the Claimant under physical and financial duress" and had been a result of "coercion" and "inadmissible pressure".[97]

6. The role of investor conduct

Investor conduct has emerged as a relevant factor in the analysis of FET claims by arbitral tribunals.[98] It may be relevant in two ways. First, it may justify the measure taken against the investor by the respondent country. Thus in *Genin v. Estonia*, the tribunal found that the Estonian national bank had good reasons to revoke the operating licence of the claimant's investment because the claimant had failed to disclose relevant facts.[99] In such cases, the adverse measure serves as a State's reaction to, or a sanction for the investor's conduct. A tribunal would need to verify that the measure at issue is indeed connected to the conduct concerned and that it does not serve as a disguise for arbitrariness or discrimination.

Fraud or misrepresentation on the part of an investor may form the basis of a legitimate regulatory interference with its rights. In such cases, even the outright termination of the investment may be justified, provided it is a proportionate response to the investor's conduct in light of the relevant domestic laws of the host State. *Azinian v. Mexico* provides an example.[100] The claimants were United States citizens who had formed a Mexican entity, DESONA, which held a concession contract to undertake waste collection and disposal in the city of Naucalpan de Juarez. The investors had obtained the concession on the basis of a business plan that asserted, among other matters, the extensive competence of the claimants in the waste management business working through a United States company named Global Waste, and which made extensive claims as to amounts of capital that would be invested and the number of jobs created.[101] In fact, only one of the investors had any experience at all in this field, and Global Waste had been in existence for only 14 months in Los Angeles, despite assertions that it had over 40 years of experience in the business.[102] In addition, the business plan relied on commitments from third parties that did not materialize. Indeed, the claimants had no resources of their own that could be used to put the plan into operation[103] and they had failed to disclose to the relevant authorities that a major third party had withdrawn from the project. The tribunal held that this non-disclosure was unconscionable.[104] More generally, the tribunal said that the local authority charged with regulating the concession contract was entitled to expect more from the investors than that they would get from third parties to carry out bits and pieces of this valuable contract once it had been signed.[105] Therefore, the termination of the concession was justifiable in the circumstances, a conclusion that had been upheld by three levels of Mexican administrative and judicial bodies.[106]

Further, in some situations, an investor's own conduct may be held to be a cause for the harm suffered. As noted above, this was the situation in *MTD Equity v. Chile,* where the investor's lack of due diligence in failing to assess correctly the lawfulness of its proposed property development, was held to account for 50 per cent of its loss. The remainder of the harm was held to be caused by the host government's unlawful actions.

The investor may bring the failure of an investment onto itself by bad management. For example in *Noble Ventures Inc v. Romania,*[107] the tribunal held that the claimant could not establish that Romania had breached the FET standard, or the expropriation provision, under the Romania-United States BIT. The claimant had invested in the privatization of a major iron and steel works, CSR, located in the Resita region, which employed some 4,000 workers. The claimant alleged, inter alia, that the respondent country had undermined the economic viability of the investment due to the failure of the relevant privatization authorities to secure the restructuring of CSR's debts, and by reason of its subsequent legal proceedings, to effect a judicial reorganization of the company. The tribunal rejected these claims by reference to the investor's conduct. It held that Noble Ventures was as much to blame for this situation as the State privatization authority.[108] Given that, in addition, the judicial reorganization of CSR had been carried out without arbitrariness or discrimination, and had not been aimed at rescinding the Privatization Agreement between the parties, it was neither deemed a breach of the FET standard, nor was it an expropriation of the claimant's investment.[109]

7. Liability threshold: Deferential standard of review

The standard of review of governmental conduct that applies to FET claims is an important, sometimes decisive factor. Essentially, it is concerned with establishing a threshold that the challenged conduct needs to exceed in order to be held in breach of the FET obligation. Existing arbitral practice shows that, in general, tribunals are reluctant to find violations lightly. Two approaches need to be distinguished however in this regard.

A high threshold has been emphasized in the context of application of the minimum standard of treatment under customary international law. The classic early tests of the MST required a violation to be "egregious" or "shocking" from the international perspective. Even though the world has moved on, and the understanding of what can be considered egregious or shocking has changed, these terms still convey a message that only very serious instances of unfair conduct can be held in breach of the MST.

The early NAFTA decision in *S.D. Myers v. Canada* underscored that the State's conduct must be "unacceptable from the international perspective. That determination must be made in the light of the **high measure of deference** that international law generally extends to the right of domestic authorities to regulate matters within their own borders" [emphasis added].[110] The tribunal stated more specifically:

> *"When interpreting and applying the "minimum standard", a Chapter 11 tribunal does not have an open-ended mandate to second-guess government decision-making. Governments have to make many potentially controversial choices. In doing so, they may appear to have made mistakes, to have misjudged the facts, proceeded on the basis of a misguided economic or sociological theory, placed too much emphasis on some social values over others and adopted solutions that are ultimately ineffective or counterproductive."[111]*

In the tribunal's opinion, such deficiencies in governmental decision-making do not provide grounds for finding an FET violation. Similarly, the *Glamis* tribunal opined that a breach of the customary law MST, as is currently stands, "still requires acts that exhibit a **high level** of shock, arbitrariness, unfairness or discrimination"[112] [emphasis added]. The tribunal further ruled that "a breach requires something greater than mere arbitrariness, something that is surprising, shocking, or exhibits a manifest lack of reasoning".[113] The Cargill tribunal stated that MST-inconsistent conduct must amount to "gross misconduct" going "beyond a merely inconsistent or questionable application of administrative or legal policy or procedure so as to constitute an unexpected and shocking repudiation of a policy's very purpose and goals, or otherwise grossly subverts a domestic law or policy for an ulterior motive".[114] These tribunals have found that a relevant violation must be "manifest", "gross", "evident", "blatant", "complete"[115] – these qualifiers point to the high liability threshold.

A second approach, using a somewhat lower threshold, has been taken by tribunals applying an unqualified FET standard (the one not linked to the customary law MST). These tribunals have – albeit to a lesser extent – also tended to express a significant degree of deference for the conduct of sovereign States. Some awards expressly state that the threshold for finding a violation is a "high one";[116] in others this is implicit in the reasoning. In *Eastern Sugar v. Czech Republic*, the tribunal emphasized that the host State is entitled to some measure of inefficiency, trial and error, and imperfection and, on this basis, found no violation.[117] In *AES v. Hungary*, the tribunal stated:

> "[I]t is not every process failing or imperfection that will amount to a failure to provide fair and equitable treatment. The standard is not one of perfection. It is only when a State's acts or procedural omissions are, on the facts and in the context before the adjudicator, manifestly unfair or unreasonable [...] that the standard can be said to have been infringed."[118]

A number of tribunals have held that a violation by the host State of an investment contract or of its own domestic law does not necessarily amount to a breach of the FET standard.[119] In a way, the standard may be compared to the prohibition of denial of justice where only gross or manifest instances of injustice are considered denials of justice and a simple error, misinterpretation or misapplication of domestic law is not (see section III.B.3). An "aberrant decision by an official lower in the hierarchy, which is capable of being reconsidered, does not of itself amount to an unlawful act" (Crawford, 1999, p. 34). The conduct concerned must implicate the State as a whole, not just one or two malevolent officials, although this does not mean that a claimant must exhaust local remedies before initiating an international arbitration.[120] International tribunals are not applying domestic standards of judicial review; a serious breach must be shown.

Tribunals have generally been strict in requiring solid evidence of States' misconduct, particular its gravest forms such as corruption, intimidation or harassment of investors. For instance, in *Tokios Tokelės v. Ukraine*, the tribunal stated that while a deliberate State campaign to punish an investor for printing materials opposed to the governing regime would clearly violate the treaty, in that case the relevant State conduct had a credible legitimate explanation other than a concerted, malicious and politically inspired campaign.[121] The *EDF* tribunal accepted that solicitation of a bribe would violate the FET standard, but stated that the alleged corruption must be substantiated by clear and convincing evidence, which was lacking in that case.[122]

However, as with many legal issues, it is impossible to set a clear benchmark that would make the application of the FET standard a mechanical operation, hence predictable to assess. At the same time, the emerging consensus on the issue of a high threshold of liability provides assurance to host States that they will not be exposed to international responsibility for minor malfunctioning of their agencies and that only manifest and flagrant acts of maladministration will be punished.

8. Damages for FET breaches

Apart from the question of establishing whether a State has breached the FET standard, there is also a question of damages due for such breaches. Investment treaties typically set out an explicit standard of compensation for expropriation cases only – most frequently, IIAs require prompt, adequate and effective compensation equal to the fair market value of the expropriated investment. When non-expropriatory treaty violations are found, damages have been awarded in accordance with the rules of international law that require "full compensation".[123] In a number of cases concerning FET breaches, this resulted in an award of the fair market value of the investment calculated by reference to future cash flows.[124]

While the question of liability is ultimately black and white – either there is a breach or not – the compensation stage potentially allows additional room for balancing of relevant interests. This balancing would be facilitated if a tribunal had flexibility to adjust the amount of compensation in light of the circumstances of the case, in particular if it could award less than full compensation where the measure, while eventually breaching the FET standard, is at least partially explained by legitimate considerations or there are other mitigating circumstances. This has already been done in cases where the tribunals found that the claimant's own conduct had contributed to the damage.[125]

It would thus appear to be beneficial if the treaty allowed tribunals to take into account case-specific equitable considerations when measuring compensation. Furthermore, in order to ensure that the host State pays an award without seriously undermining the general welfare of its population, future profits may be excluded from any compensation for FET breaches (see section IV, policy option 4). These issues call for further exploration and possible reflection in IIAs.

C. Summary and implications for international investment treaties

There is no full consistency in the application and interpretation by arbitral tribunals of the FET obligation. Indeed, it would be difficult to expect such consistency in a system where numerous one-off arbitral tribunals adjudicate disputes under a variety of differently formulated standards and factual situations and furthermore in the absence of an effective appellate review.

At the same time, one can discern some emerging trends from a significant set of arbitral opinions. Firstly, it is becoming apparent that the clarification of the FET standard by reference to its source – in particular, by reference to the minimum standard of treatment under customary international law – is likely to lead to a stricter and narrower interpretation of the standard. However, this result is not guaranteed – the "evolutionary" view, taken by a number of tribunals, provides an avenue for a more generous reading. Secondly, a *de facto* convergence has been taking place between the qualified and unqualified FET standards as far as the main substantive elements of the standard are concerned. The difference between the two expressions of the standard is that the liability threshold under an unqualified FET standard will be somewhat lower than under the qualified one. Nevertheless, on the whole, arbitral interpretation demonstrates that a violation of fair and equitable treatment can be found only where the acts of State misconduct are rather grave and manifest, even where the applicable FET clause is an unqualified one.

The significant number of decided cases has generated some salient trends clarifying the content of the FET standard. As discussed above, these include the limited protection of investors' legitimate expectations, a prohibition of arbitrary and discriminatory treatment, denial of justice and abusive conduct towards investors. Other elements, such as transparency, consistency, legality and stability of regulatory framework, have featured in a number of arbitral awards, but it appears premature to speak about a consensus in relation to those, given the concern and criticism they have raised and the fact that some of those them were drawn from the preamble of the applicable treaty and not from the FET obligation itself.

Based on recent cases, it can also be deduced that the investor's own conduct is a factor in determining whether an FET breach has occurred. This particularly refers to instances of unconscionable conduct that justify adverse measures against the investment as well as to the obligation to undertake an independent due diligence and proper investment planning.

A number of arbitral awards display a risk that tribunals may evaluate the FET standard only in terms of an investor's expectations, without due consideration given to a State's wider political and social obligations, although on the whole, tribunals have paid attention to distinguishing legitimate regulation from governmental conduct that violates the standard. As noted in section I, "fairness" and "equity" should be read as referring to all classes of actors affected by a particular decision or procedure, not just one category. While IIAs are undoubtedly negotiated to protect investors, they also create an environment for the development of host countries by way of attracting and benefitting from investment. Furthermore, they are not meant to protect investors to the detriment of the host country's economy and population. The more recent awards appear to accept this approach. The challenge for IIA negotiators is to enshrine this in new treaty language or use it to clarify existing treaty provisions

The practice regarding fair and equitable treatment is in a state of development. As new cases and fact patterns appear, tribunals will face new questions. The existing questions will also continue to be addressed, with a possibility that the application of the standard will become more predictable. The comparative law methodology seeking to identify common principles of national laws applicable to State administration and governance (for example, Schill, 2010) can prove helpful in this regard. With time, it is hoped, a broader consensus will emerge on the sources, scope and content of the FET standard.

States should actively influence and shape the relevant practice. Indeed, as the authors of investment treaties and creators of international law, governments should continue considering how to formulate the FET obligation – or provide an agreed interpretation to existing fair and equitable treatment clauses – in a way that would guide the tribunals and address existing and future problems of its application. To assist in this task, the next section of this paper considers a variety of options for negotiators and policymakers.

Notes

[1] *LFH Neer and Pauline Neer v Mexico (US v Mexico)* (1926) 4 RIAA 60, pp. 61-62 [emphasis added].

[2] *S.D. Myers, Inc. v. Government of Canada*, UNCITRAL (NAFTA) Partial Award, 13 November 2000, para. 263 [emphasis added].

[3] *Waste Management v. Mexico*, ICSID Case No ARB(AF)/00/3, Award, 30 April 2004, 43 ILM 967 (2004), para. 98 [emphasis added].

[4] Ibid., para. 99.

[5] *GAMI Investments Inc. v. Mexico*, UNCITRAL (NAFTA), Final Award, 15 November 2004, para. 97.

[6] *International Thunderbird Gaming Corporation v. Mexico*, UNCITRAL (NAFTA), Award, 26 January 2006.

[7] *Cargill v. Mexico*, ICSID Case No. ARB(AF)/05/2, Award, 18 September 2009, paras. 284–285.

[8] *Glamis Gold, Ltd. v. United States*, UNCITRAL (NAFTA), Award, 8 June 2009.

[9] *ADF Group Inc v. United States*, ICSID Case No ARB(AF)/00/1, Award, 9 January 2003, para. 190

[10] The *UPS v. Canada* case exemplifies the second prong of this test: in that case the claimant alleged that NAFTA Article 1105 had been infringed by Canada through its failure to ensure fair competition in the market for non-monopoly postal services. The Article 1105 claim was held to be outside the tribunal's jurisdiction on the grounds that "there is no rule of

customary international law prohibiting or regulation anti-competitive behaviour", *UPS v. Canada*, UNCITRAL Rules, Award on Jurisdiction, 22 November 2002, para. 92.

[11] *Merrill & Ring v. Canada*, UNCITRAL Rules, Award, 31 March 2010.

[12] Ibid., para. 211.

[13] Ibid., para. 213.

[14] Note that even this – apparently the most conservative approach to the interpretation of the minimum standard of treatment of aliens – goes beyond the orthodox view of the standard as limited to the obligations to accord police protection and security and not to deny justice.

[15] This approach seems to contradict the 2001 Interpretative Note, whose rationale was to draw a clear line between the minimum standard of treatment of aliens under customary law and an unqualified obligation to grant fair and equitable treatment.

[16] See, in particular, *M.C.I. Power Group L.C. and New Turbine, Inc. v. Ecuador*, ICSID Case No. ARB/03/6, Award, 31 July 2007, para. 369; *Siemens AG v. Argentina*, ICSID Case No ARB/02/8, Award, 6 February 2007, para. 291; *Genin v. Estonia*, ICSID Case No. ARB/99/2, Award, 25 June 2001, para. 367; *Occidental Exploration and Production Co v. Ecuador*, LCIA Case No. UN 3467, Award, 1 July 2004, paras. 189–190.

[17] See, for example, *Compañía de Aguas del Aconquija S.A. and Vivendi Universal S.A. v. Argentina*, ICSID Case No. ARB/97/3, Award, 20 August 2007, paras. 7.4.5, 7.4.9, and 7.4.12; *Tecmed v. Mexico*, ICSID Case No. ARB(AF)/00/2, Award, 29 May 2003, para. 154; *Enron v. Argentina*, ICSID Case No. ARB/01/3, Award, 22 May 2007, paras. 258–259; *Lemire v. Ukraine*, ICSID Case No. ARB/06/18, Decision on Jurisdiction and Liability, 21 January 2010, paras. 253–254.

[18] For example, *ATA Construction v. Jordan*, Award, 18 May 2010; *Helnan v. Egypt*, Award, 3 July 2008 and others.

[19] *Rumeli Telekom v. Kazakhstan*, ICSID Case No. ARB/05/16, Award, 29 July 2008, para. 611; *Biwater Gauff v. Tanzania*, ICSID Case No ARB/05/22, Award, 24 July 2008, para. 592; *Duke Energy v. Ecuador*, ICSID Case No. ARB/04/19, Award, 18 August 2008, para. 337; *Saluka v. Czech Republic*, UNCITRAL, Partial Award, 17 March 2006, para. 291; *Azurix v. Argentina*, ICSID Case No. ARB/01/12, Final Award, 14 July

2006, para. 361; *CMS v. Argentine Republic*, ICSID Case No. ARB/01/8, Award, 12 May 2005, paras. 282–284; and *Occidental v. Ecuador*, LCIA Administered Case No. UN 3467, Award, 1 July 2004, para. 190.

[20] *Biwater Gauff v. Tanzania*, ICSID Case No ARB/05/22, Award, 24 July 2008, paras. 591 and 596–599; *Jan de Nul v. Egypt*, ICSID Case No. ARB/04/13, Award, 6 November 2008, paras. 187 and 192–194; *EDF v. Romania*, ICSID Case No. ARB/05/13, Award, 8 October 2009, para. 216; *Azurix v.Argentina*, Final Award, 14 July 2006, paras. 368–370; and others.

[21] *Biwater Gauff (Tanzania) Ltd. v. United Republic of Tanzania*, ICSID Case No. ARB/05/22, Award, 24 July 2008, para. 597.

[22] *Saluka v. Czech Republic*, UNCITRAL, Partial Award, 17 March 2006, para. 293 [emphasis added].

[23] See *MCI v. Ecuador,* Award, 31 July 2007, para. 302; *Saluka v. Czech Republic*, UNCITRAL, Partial Award, 17 March 2006, para. 284; *SD Myers v. Canada,* First Partial Award, 13 November 2000, para. 261; *ADF v. United States*, Award, 9 January 2003, para. 184; *Mondev v. United States*, Award, 11 October 2002, para. 119; see also Schreuer, 2005, p. 365.

[24] On "transparency", see Newcombe and Paradell, 2009, pp. 291–294; and Salacuse, 2010, pp. 237–238. On "consistency", see Vandevelde, 2010, p. 66 *et seq.*

[25] *The Oxford English Dictionary* (1989), Second Edition, Clarendon Press, Oxford, vol. I, p. 602.

[26] The *Saluka* tribunal stated that the term "measures" covers any action or omission of the host State referring to the ICJ's decision in the *Fisheries Jurisdiction Case (Spain v. Canada)* where the ICJ found that the term is "wide enough to cover any act, step or proceeding". See *Saluka v. Czech Republic,* UNCITRAL, Partial Award, 17 March 2006, para. 459. On the term "treatment" in the MFN context, see UNCTAD (2010), pp.15–17.

[27] See Kinnear, 2008 and references therein. However, this is not a universally shared opinion. For a fierce critique of legitimate expectation denying the place of this concept in the FET standard, see Judge Nikken's separate opinion in *AWG Group v. Argentina*, UNCITRAL, Decision on Liability, 30 July 2010.

[28] *Occidental v. Ecuador*, LCIA Case No. UN 3467, Final Award, 1 July 2004, para. 183; *Enron v. Argentina*, ICSID Case No. ARB/01/3, Award, 22 May 2007, para. 260.

[29] *CMS v. Argentina*, Award of 12 May 2005, para. 274; *Enron v. Argentina*, Award of 22 May 2007, paras. 259–260.

[30] Ibid., paras.264–268.

[31] Ibid., para. 268. The findings of the *Enron* tribunal were later reviewed by the ICSID Annulment Committee. The Committee found, in relation to the tribunal's interpretation of the FET standard, that the tribunal had not manifestly exceeded its powers. See *Enron v. Argentina*, Decision on the Application for Annulment, 30 July 2010, paras. 298–316.

[32] *PSEG Global et al. v. Republic of Turkey*, ICSID Case No. ARB/02/5, Award, 19 January 2007, paras. 252–253. However, the same tribunal also stated that "[l]egitimate expectations by definition require a **promise of the administration** on which the claimants rely to assert a right that needs to be observed" (para. 241) [emphasis added], which suggests that the commitment needs to be specific.

[33] *Occidental Exploration and Production Co v. Ecuador*, LCIA Case No. UN 3467, Final Award, 1 July 2004, para. 190.

[34] Ibid., para. 196.

[35] *Duke Energy v. Ecuador*, ICSID Case No. ARB/04/19, Award, August 18, 2008, para. 340.

[36] See, for instance, *Continental Casualty v. Argentina*, ICSID Case No.ARB/03/9, Award, 5 September 2008, where the tribunal describes relevant factors at para. 261.

[37] *Methanex Corporation v. United States of America*, UNCITRAL, (NAFTA), Final Award, 3 August 2005.

[38] Ibid., at Part IV, Chapter D, page 5, para 7.

[39] Stabilization clauses should be treated with caution, given the controversial nature of such clauses and the fact that, in practice, they have been used to prevent the application of socially important laws, such as environmental and human rights law, to investors. See Shemberg, 2008. Whether IIAs should be used to uphold such clauses is open to debate.

[40] See *Glamis Gold, Ltd. v. United States*, UNCITRAL (NAFTA), Award, 8 June 2009, para. 627.

[41] *Enron v. Argentina,* ICSID Case No. ARB/01/3, Award, 22 May 2007, paras. 264–266; *LG&E v. Argentina,* ICSID Case No. ARB/02/1, Award, 25 July 2007, paras. 130 and 133.

[42] *Metalpar v. Argentina,* ICSID Case No. ARB/03/5, Award on the Merits, 6 June 2008, para. 186.

[43] *CMS v. Argentina,* ICSID Case No. ARB/01/8, Award, 12 May 2005, para. 277.

[44] Ibid., para. 275.

[45] Kinnear, 2008, p. 227, referring to *Enron v. Argentina,* Award, 22 May 2007, para. 262; *CME Czech Republic BV (The Netherlands) v. Czech Republic,* UNCITRAL, Partial Award, 13 September 2001, para. 611; *Tecmed v. Mexico,* Award, 29 May 2003, para 154; *LG&E v. Argentina,* Award, 25 July 2007, para. 127. For example, in *Continental Casualty v. Argentina,* the tribunal dismissed the FET claim inter alia because the general legislative provisions had not been "the basis on which Continental had relied in making its investment in Argentina" (para. 259).

[46] *Parkerings-Compagniet AS v. Lithuania,* ICSID Case No. ARB/05/8, Award, 11 September 2007, para. 344.

[47] *Hamester v. Ghana,* ICSID Case No. ARB/07/24, Award, 18 June 2010, para. 337.

[48] Ibid., paras. 244–246.

[49] *Bayindir v. Pakistan,* ICSID Case No ARB/03/29, Award, 27 August 2009, para. 190; *Duke Energy v. Ecuador,* ICSID Case No. ARB/04/19, Award, 18 August 2008, para. 340; *AES v. Hungary,* ICSID Case No. ARB/02/17, Award, 23 September 2010, paras.9.3.8–9.3.12.

[50] See *Kardassopoulos v. Georgia,* ICSID Case No. ARB/05/18, Award, 10 March 2010, paras. 434–441.

[51] See *Methanex v. United States,* Final Award, 3 August 2005, Part IV, Chapter D, para. 10.

[52] See *Generation Ukraine, Inc v. Ukraine,* ICSID No. ARB/00/9, Award, 16 September 2003, paras. 20.37.

[53] *Genin v. Estonia,* ICSID Case No. ARB/99/2, Award, 25 June 2001, para. 348.

[54] *Parkerings-Compagniet AS v. Lithuania,* ICSID Case No. ARB/05/8, Award, 11 September 2007, paras. 335–336.

[55] Relevant case law is reviewed in Newcombe and Paradell, 2009, pp. 291–294; as well as in Salacuse, 2010, pp. 237–238.

[56] *Saluka v. Czech Republic,* UNCITRAL Rules, Partial Award, 17 March 2006.

[57] Ibid., paras. 304-308.

[58] See also *Joseph C. Lemire v. Ukraine*, ICSID Case No. ARB/06/18, Decision on Jurisdiction and Liability, 21 January 2010 ("[T]he object and purpose of the Treaty [Ukraine-United States BIT] is not to protect foreign investments per se, but as an aid to the development of the domestic economy. And local development requires that the preferential treatment of foreigners be balanced against the legitimate right of Ukraine to pass legislation and adopt measures for the protection of what as a sovereign it perceives to be its public interest.")

[59] *Parkerings-Compagniet AS v. Lithuania*, ICSID Case No. ARB/05/8, Award, 11 September 2007, paras. 334–338.

[60] Ibid., para. 332.

[61] *Continental Casualty v. Argentina*, ICSID Case No. ARB/03/9, Award, 5 September 2008, para. 258.

[62] Ibid.

[63] Kinnear, 2008, p. 225, referring to *Vivendi v. Argentina II*, ICSID Case No. ARB/97/3, Award, 20 August 2007, para.7.4.31.

[64] *EDF v. Romania*, ICSID Case No. ARB/05/13, Award, 8 October 2009.

[65] Ibid., para. 217.

[66] Ibid., para. 219.

[67] Ibid., paras. 221 and 237.

[68] For details, see ibid., paras. 240–301.

[69] Ibid., paras. 293–294.

[70] *Oxford English Dictionary*, 1989, Second Edition, Clarendon Press, Oxford, vol. XVIII, p. 464.

[71] *Lauder v. Czech Republic,* UNCITRAL, Award, 3 September 2001, para. 221; *Plama Consortium Limited v. Bulgaria*, ICSID Case No. ARB/03/24, Award, 27 August 2008, para. 184. Existing awards have mostly analysed arbitrariness in the context of separate BIT obligation that prohibits arbitrary measures. However, tribunals have often emphasized that prohibition of arbitrariness is part and parcel of the FET standard.

[72] In *Lemire*, the tribunal stated that "the underlying notion of arbitrariness is that prejudice, preference or bias is substituted for the rule of law" (*Joseph C. Lemire v. Ukraine*, ICSID Case No. ARB/06/18, Decision on Jurisdiction and Liability, 21 January 2010, para. 385.)

[73] *Elettronica Sicula SpA (United States of America v. Italy)*, Judgment, 29 July 1989, *I.C.J. Reports* 1989, p. 15.

[74] *Enron v. Argentina*, ICSID Case No. ARB/01/3, Award, 22 May 2007, para. 281.

[75] *LG&E v. Argentina*, ICSID Case No. ARB/02/1, Decision on Liability, 3 October 2006, para. 162.

[76] *AES v. Hungary*, ICSID Case No. ARB/02/17, Award, 23 September 2010, paras. 10.3.31 and 10.3.34.

[77] Arbitrariness "is a willful disregard of due process of law, act which shocks, or at least surprises a sense of judicial propriety" (*Elettronica Sicula SpA (United States v. Italy)*, Judgment, 29 July 1989, *I.C.J. Reports* 1989, p.15). See also *Loewen v. United States,* ICSID Case No. ARB(AF)98/3, Award, 26 June 2003, para. 131; *Genin v. Estonia*, ICSID Case No. ARB/99/2, Award, 25 June 2001, para. 371.

[78] *Joseph C. Lemire v. Ukraine*, ICSID Case No. ARB/06/18, Decision on Jurisdiction and Liability, 21 January 2010, para. 385.

[79] See the 1929 Harvard draft codification, Responsibility of States for damage done in their territory to the person or property of foreigners, in the *American Journal of International Law*, Special Supplement 131, vol. 23, 1929 (Article 9).

[80] Ibid., and accompanying references to international authorities.

[81] For instance, in *Petrobart v. Kyrgyz Republic*, the tribunal held that the collusion between the executive and the court constituted "a clear breach of the prohibition of denial of justice under international law" (Award, 13 February 2003, p. 28).

[82] *Loewen v. United States,* ICSID Case No. ARB(AF)98/3, Award, 26 June 2003, para. 135.

[83] Focarelli (2009). See, for example, *Pantechniki v. Albania*, ICSID Case No. ARB/07/21, Award, 30 July 2009, paras. 96-97; *Jan de Nul v Egypt*, Award, 6 November 2008, paras. 255–259.

[84] J. Crawford, Special Rapporteur to the International Law Commission, *Second Report on State Responsibility*, 17 March 1999, UN Doc A/CN 4/498, para. 75. See also Paulsson 2006, pp. 100 et seq.

[85] *Jan de Nul v. Egypt*, Award, 6 November 2008, para. 204.

[86] See, for example, ASEAN Comprehensive Investment Agreement (2009), Article 11.

[87] In this context, the due process requirement appears to be independent from denial of justice and thus there is no need to exhaust local remedies.

[88] In *Metalclad*, the tribunal noted, as one factor in finding a violation of FET, that the construction permit was denied to the claimant "at a meeting of the Municipal Town Council of which Metalclad received no notice, to which it received no invitation and at which it was given no opportunity to appear" (*Metalclad v. Mexico*, Award, 30 August 2000, paras. 91 and 97).

[89] In *Genin v. Estonia*, the tribunal established certain procedural violations on the part of the Bank of Estonia that revoked the licence from the claimant's local bank (no formal notice of revocation or grace period to comply with the Central bank's requirements, no invitation to the session where the decision to revoke the licence had been taken, immediate effect of the decision to revoke). However, given that the revocation was found to be a reasonable regulatory decision, the tribunal did not find a breach of the FET standard (*Genin v.Estonia*, Award, 25 June 2001, paras. 363–365). As noted in *GAMI v. Mexico*, "Proof of a good faith effort by the Government to achieve the objectives of its laws and regulations may counterbalance instances of disregard of legal or regulatory requirements" (Final Award, 15 November 2004, para. 97)

[90] *Saluka v. Czech Republic*. Partial Award, 17 March 2006, para. 461; *Loewen v. United States*, Award on Merits, 26 June 2003, para. 123; *Waste Management, Inc. v. Mexico*, ICSID Case No. ARB(AF)/00/3, Award, 30 April 2004, para. 98; and *CMS v. Argentina*, Award, 12 May 2005, para. 287.

[91] *Glamis v. United States*, Award, 8 June 2009, footnote 1087 to para. 542; *Waste Management v. Mexico*, Final Award, 30 April 2004, para. 138.

[92] *Grand River Enterprises v. United States*, Award, 12 January 2011, para.209.

[93] *Eureko v. Poland*, Partial Award, 19 August 2005, para. 237.

[94] *Waste Management v. Mexico*, Final Award, 30 April 2004, para. 138.

[95] *PSEG v. Turkey*, Award, 19 January 2007, para. 245. It was also noted in *GAMI v. Mexico* that "[t]he record as a whole—not isolated events—determines whether there has been a breach of international law." (Final Award, 15 November 2004, para. 97).

[96] *Saluka v. Czech Republic*, Partial Award, 17 March 2006, para. 308.

[97] *Desert Line Projects LLC v. Yemen*, ICSID Case No. ARB/05/17, Award, 6 February 2008. paras. 179, 185–187, 190 and 193. See also *Pope and Talbot v. Canada,* where the tribunal found instances of unfounded "threats of reductions and even termination of the Investment's export quotas, suggestions of criminal investigations of the Investment's conduct" (Award on Damages, 31 May 2002, para. 68).

[98] See further Muchlinski, 2006.

[99] *Genin v. Estonia*, ICSID Case No. ARB/99/2, Award, 25 June 2001, para. 362.

[100] *Azinian v. Mexico*, ICSID Case No. ARB(AF)/97/2, Award, 1 November 1999.

[101] Ibid., para. 106.

[102] Ibid., para. 29.

[103] Ibid., para. 33.

[104] Ibid., para. 110.

[105] Ibid., paras. 114–115.

[106] It may be noted that similar considerations of the need to control unconscionable conduct of the investor have motivated tribunals to find that an investment had not been made in accordance with host country laws and therefore should not benefit from the BIT protection. For example, in *Fraport v. The Philippines*, Award, 16 August 2007, the tribunal refused jurisdiction because the claimant had deliberately sought to evade nationality of ownership requirements under local law.

[107] *Noble Ventures v. Romania*, ICSID Case No.ARB/01/11, Award, 12 October 2005. A similar analysis motivated the ICJ to reject a United States claim against Italy under the Italy-United States Friendship, Commerce and Navigation Treaty, which had alleged the arbitrary deprivation of property belonging to United States parent companies, when the Italian local authorities in Sicily nationalized the local subsidiary

owned and controlled by the United States parent companies. The ICJ found that mismanagement by the United States parent companies had motivated the taking and that this was done to avert a social catastrophe in a deprived region of Italy: *ELSI Case (Case Concerning Elettronica Sicula S.p.A (ELSI) United States v. Italy, I.C.J. Reports* 1989). See for discussion Muchlinski, 2006, pp. 548–549.

[108] *Noble Ventures v. Romania* ICSID Case No. ARB/01/11, Award, 12 October 2005, para. 137 et seq.

[109] Ibid., paras. 175–183.

[110] *S.D. Myer v. Canada*, Partial Award, 13 November 2000, para. 263.

[111] Ibid., para. 261. Quoted with approval in *Cargill v. Mexico*, ICSID Case No. ARB(AF)/05/2, Award, 18 September 2009, para. 292.

[112] *Glamis v. United States*, Award, 8 June 2009, para. 829.

[113] Ibid., para. 617.

[114] *Cargill v. Mexico*, ICSID Case No. ARB(AF)/05/2, Award, 18 September 2009, paras. 286 and 296.

[115] *Glamis v. United States*, Award, 8 June 2009, para. 616; *Cargill v. Mexico*, Award, 18 September 2009, para. 285.

[116] *Biwater v. Tanzania*, Award, 24 July 2008, para. 597.

[117] *Eastern Sugar B.V. v. Czech Republic*, SCC Case No. 088/2004, Partial Award, 27 March 2007, para. 272. The tribunal also noted, however, that governmental interference does not necessarily have to be "blatant or outrageous" to lead to a violation.

[118] *AES v Hungary*, Award, 23 September 2010, para. 9.3.40.

[119] *Parkerings-Compagniet v. Lithuania*, Award, 11 September 2007, para. 315; *Biwater v. Tanzania*, Award, 24 July 2008, paras. 635–636; *RFCC v. Morocco*, ICSID Case No. ARB/00/6, Award, 22 December 2003, para. 48; *Waste Management v. Mexico*, Final Award, 30 April 2004, para. 115; *Duke Energy v. Ecuador*, ICSID Case No. ARB/04/19, Award, 18 August 2008, para. 342; *Bayindir v. Pakistan*, Award, 27 August 2009, paras. 123–139, 180. See also *Elettronica Sicula SpA (United States v. Italy)*, ICJ Judgment, 29 July 1989, *I.C.J. Reports* 1989, p. 15.

[120] As one tribunal noted, albeit in the expropriation context: "it is not enough for an investor to seize upon an act of maladministration, no matter how low the level of the relevant governmental authority; to abandon his

investment without any effort at overturning the administrative fault [...]. In such instances, an international tribunal may deem that the failure to seek redress from national authorities disqualifies the international claim" (*Generation Ukraine v. Ukraine*, Award, 16 September 2003, para. 20.30.).

[121] *Tokios Tokelės v. Ukraine*, ICSID Case No. ARB/02/18, Award, 26 July 2007, paras. 123 and 136.

[122] *EDF v. Romania*, ICSID Case No. ARB/05/13, Award, 18 October 2009, para. 221.

[123] See Ripinsky with Williams, 2008, pp. 88–90.

[124] *CMS v. Argentina*, Award, 12 May 2005; *Enron v. Argentina*, Award of 22 May 2007; *Sempra Energy v. Argentina*, Award, 28 September 2007; *British Gas v. Argentina*, Final Award, 24 December 2007.

[125] *MTD v. Chile*, Award of 25 May 2004; *Azurix v. Argentina*, Award, 14 July 2006.

IV. OPTIONS FOR NEGOTIATORS AND POLICYMAKERS

In light of the foregoing discussion and the current lack of predictability, the principal aim for negotiators in relation to the FET standard should be to clarify the source and the content of the obligation, and by doing so, to determine the degree of discretion that the contracting parties want to leave to the arbitral tribunal that will be asked to interpret the provision. In this regard, negotiators have a variety of choices and will need to decide whether they want to leave a high degree of interpretative discretion to the arbitral tribunal or whether they want to determine in the treaty itself the source and elements of content when referring to the FET standard. In addition, there is a broad range of policy choices available that take into account the priorities of negotiators and a desirable balance between a broad investor-protection-focussed standard and a more narrow formulation that seeks to preserve primarily the State's interests, while ensuring the investor has adequate protection against major forms of maladministration.

A clearer, qualified and/or more specific language of FET clauses can be used not only in the newly concluded IIAs and countries' model BITs. It may equally be introduced through additional protocols or annexes to a treaty, as well as interpretative instruments, such as notes of interpretation agreed by the parties. (See UNCTAD, 2011.)

The vagueness of the FET standard, as currently expressed in the majority of IIAs, is the main reason for a lack of consistency in its interpretation. Some may treat this as a desirable flexibility in order for the standard to cover a limitless variety of situations; however, "one treaty interpreter's flexibility is another treaty interpreter's chaos" (Kinnear, 2008, p. 237). Even though there are signs of emerging substantive content of the standard (see section III.B), the extent of host State exposure to potential liability is still uncertain. Given the possibility for tribunals to provide unexpectedly wide interpretations of the standard that may go beyond the actual intention of the parties, the clarity of drafting is paramount. A number of options can be identified.

Option 1: No reference to FET

Existing IIAs rarely omit the FET standard, although there are several examples to the contrary (see section II.B). The more common response to the risks of an overbroad application of the standard has been to draft the FET provision in a more restricted manner. Even in the absence of an FET clause, a host State must treat foreign investments in accordance with the minimum standard of treatment of aliens because it can be argued that this standard is part of customary international law, which applies regardless of specific treaty obligations. Whether an investor would be able to use the ISDS mechanism to enforce the minimum standard of treatment of aliens is another question. This would not be possible if an IIA limits the jurisdiction of arbitral tribunals solely to those claims where a breach of the treaty is alleged. In contrast, arbitral tribunals should be able to adjudicate claims relating to the minimum standard of treatment under those treaties that have broad ISDS clauses, for example, encompassing "any disputes relating to an investment".

Option 2: Unqualified FET clause

It was noted in section II.C that a significant number of agreements have a general unqualified FET provision, that is, they contain a simple promise to accord to investment "fair and equitable treatment" without any further reference to source or content, elaboration or restrictions. The main advantage of the unqualified approach is to reassure investors that the host country is willing to subject its administrative and regulatory processes to the scrutiny of an arbitral tribunal operating outside the national legal system. However, this opens the door to an expansive approach to the review of administrative action as there is no indication in the FET provision concerning the limit of its scope and content.

A tribunal would be free to assess each claim on a case-by-case basis and to read into the wording what it feels fit to include because the contracting parties have entrusted it with this mandate. The liability threshold is potentially lower than under the FET obligation qualified by reference to the minimum standard of treatment of aliens, although this may depend on the view of a specific tribunal. The unqualified formulation is potentially the most investor-oriented option, especially when coupled with a preamble that emphasizes fair and equitable treatment or investment protection as the sole or main objective of the treaty. It gives the possibility to the tribunal to focus on the needs and perspectives of the investor and a possible underestimation of the need to balance those claims against the host country's sovereign rights and duties to regulate in the public interest.

> **Possible formulation (unqualified stand-alone obligation)**
>
> Each Contracting Party shall at all times ensure fair and equitable treatment of the investments by investors of the other Contracting Party.

Option 3(a): Linking the FET standard to the minimum standard of treatment under customary international law

It was noted in section II.E that some agreements refer to the minimum standard of treatment of aliens under customary international law (MST). A reference to the MST assumes that tribunals examining FET claims will hold the claimant to this demanding standard. In theory, to demonstrate a violation of a particular right, the claimant must first prove that the MST protects this right. To do so, it must show a sufficiently wide and representative State practice on the matter and provide evidence of opinio juris, i.e. that States follow this practice from a sense of legal obligation. In practice, however, given that the traditional MST is undeveloped and not truly adapted to modern economic realities, the test is very difficult to meet if this approach is followed literally.

Consequently, as shown in section III.A.2, some tribunals view the MST as an *evolving* standard. Nevertheless, the main feature of this approach remains a high liability threshold that outlaws only the very serious breaches. In the words of the *Glamis* tribunal, it is "a floor, an absolute bottom, below which conduct is not accepted by the international community"; it would have to be sufficiently basic to allow countries in all stages of development to conform to it.

The general reference to MST may be complemented by a closed or illustrative list of conduct that the State considers to be proscribed under the standard. Such a list may include gross denial of justice, manifest arbitrariness, a complete lack of due process, evident discrimination or a manifest lack of reasons. (See relevant formulations in policy option 4.)

Possible formulation 1 (reference to the minimum standard of treatment)

Investments or returns of investors of either Contracting Party shall at all times be accorded treatment in accordance with the customary international law minimum standard of treatment of aliens, including fair and equitable treatment.

The concept of fair and equitable treatment does not require treatment in addition to or beyond that which is required by the customary international law minimum standard of treatment of aliens.

Possible formulation 2 (reference to the minimum standard of treatment, including an obligation not to deny justice)

Each Party shall accord to covered investments treatment in accordance with customary international law, including fair and equitable treatment.

For greater certainty, paragraph 1 prescribes the customary

---

international law minimum standard of treatment of aliens as the minimum standard of treatment to be afforded to covered investments. The concepts of fair and equitable treatment does not require treatment in addition to or beyond that which is required by that standard, and do not create additional substantive rights. The obligation in paragraph 1 to provide fair and equitable treatment includes the obligation not to deny justice in criminal, civil, or administrative adjudicatory proceedings in accordance with the principle of due process embodied in the principal legal systems of the world.

Option 3(b): Linking the FET standard to international law or to principles of international law

This option is similar to option 3(a) in the sense that it also seeks to circumscribe the FET standard by reference to a source, as opposed to content. In this case, the whole body of international law serves as the relevant source. Under this approach, the disputing parties and the tribunal must derive relevant obligations of host States from general international law including, among others, the relevant general principles of national law as well as relevant decisions of international tribunals and writings of publicists.[1]

Theoretically, a reference to "international law" controls tribunal discretion less than a reference to the "customary international law minimum standard of treatment" because the former notion is significantly broader than the latter. However, arbitral practice of the past decade shows that tribunals do not strictly adhere to the process of deriving legal norms from the relevant sources.

It may be possible to take into account differences in host country characteristics and levels of development and the extent of known business risk undertaken by the investor as relevant factors. However the degree to which such specificities can influence the outcome of the claim remain unclear.

States wishing to provide additional guidance to tribunals and restrict their ability to interpret the FET standard in an overly expansive manner may therefore wish to fill it with specific elements of content. (See relevant formulations in policy option 4.)

Possible formulation 1 (general reference to international law)

Investments or returns of investors of either Contracting Party in the territory of the other Contracting Party shall be accorded fair and equitable treatment in accordance with international law [or with principles of international law].

Possible formulation 2 (international law to set the floor of protection)

Investments shall at all times be accorded fair and equitable treatment and full protection and security and shall in no case be accorded treatment less than that required by international law.

Option 4: Identifying the content of the FET standard and listing specific substantive obligations

As discussed earlier, making an explicit reference to the source of an FET obligation – be it customary law MST or general international law – has not always been effective in narrowing down arbitral discretion. The fact that the MST and the relevant rules of general international law are rather unclear has pushed tribunals towards developing their own substantive content for the FET standard.

An alternative way to qualify, clarify and/or narrow down the FET standard is to replace the general FET provision with a number of more specific obligations such as prohibition of:

(a) Denial of justice and flagrant violations of due process;

(b) Manifestly arbitrary treatment;

(c) Evident discrimination;

(d) Manifestly abusive treatment involving continuous, unjustified coercion or harassment;

(e) Infringement of legitimate expectations based on investment-inducing representations or measures, on which the investor has relied.

The list may be formulated as exhaustive, although it does not necessarily need to be limited to those elements listed above; the list of elements may be narrower or broader, depending on the wishes of the contracting parties. Importantly, the replacement of the general FET standard with specific obligations should rein in arbitrators' creativity and remove other factors and criteria that some tribunals have relied upon in order to find a violation of FET, such as transparency, consistency, legality and stability of regulatory framework. Certainly, the aforementioned obligations still leave room for the arbitrators' assessment, but it is not close to the amount of discretion that they enjoy when adjudicating under a broad and unqualified FET clause.

Possible formulation 1

1. Each Party shall abstain from treating investors and their investments in a manner that is manifestly arbitrary, discriminatory or abusive. It shall not deny justice in any legal or administrative proceedings or otherwise flagrantly violate due process.

[Neither Party shall infringe legitimate expectations based on investment-inducing representations or measures, on which the investor has relied when making an investment. In this respect, the investor's conduct and accepted business risk in the territory of the Party concerned should be taken into account when determining the legitimate expectations of the investor].

The additional use of adjectives such as "manifest", "evident", "flagrant", "continuous" and "unjustified" would convey a message that the standard of review of the governmental conduct should be deferential and that the threshold for finding a violation rather high. At the same time, the standard formulated in this manner will ensure that serious incidents of State misconduct will not go unpunished.

In fact, some investment treaties have started to introduce specific elements of the content of fair and equitable treatment, although most of them do so in addition to the general FET provision, which suggests that FET is not limited to those elements expressly listed and so does not completely remove the possibility of an expansive reading by arbitral tribunals. (On relevant IIA practice, see section II.F).

The described type of provision, as well as the traditional FET clause, could also be supplemented by further interpretative guidance, including statements to the effect that:

(a) The clause does not preclude the State from adopting regulatory or other measures that pursue legitimate policy objectives, including measures to meet other international obligations;

(b) The investor's conduct and the country's level of development and level of business risk are relevant in determining whether the clause has been breached;

(c) A breach of another provision of an IIA or of another international agreement cannot establish a claim for breach of the clause;

(d) In the event that a breach is found, the amount of compensation awarded should compensate for direct losses of the claimant, taking into account equitable considerations and other relevant circumstances of the case.

Several of these considerations have already found some support in arbitral practice, but an explicit treaty text would make them mandatory for a tribunal and will help the cause of legal certainty.

Possible formulation 2 (can be added to possible formulation 1 above)

2. This Article does not preclude the Parties from adopting regulatory or other measures that pursue legitimate policy objectives, including measures to meet other international obligations.

3. For greater certainty, different forms and levels of development of administrative, legislative and judicial systems of each Party should be taken into account in determining whether any of the obligations set out in paragraph 1 of this Article have been breached.

4. A determination that there has been a breach of another provision of this Agreement, or of a separate international agreement, does not establish that there has been a breach of this Article.

5. The amount of compensation to be paid to an investor as a result of the breach of paragraph 1 of this Article shall be equitable in light of the relevant circumstances of the case, limited to the claimant's direct losses, and may in no case exceed the amount of capital invested and interest at a commercially reasonable rate.

Option 5: Balanced treaty preamble

In addition to various forms of expressing the FET obligation (options 1–3) or replacing it with more specific obligations (option 4), policymakers may wish to ensure that, overall, the treaty does not single out investment protection as its only objective, but takes into account other legitimate and important policy considerations.

A treaty preamble typically sets out the objectives of the agreement and forms part of the agreement's context. An arbitral tribunal faced with a vague and unqualified obligation is likely to look into the preamble under the rules of interpretation of the Vienna Convention on the Law of Treaties (Article 31). It must be remembered, however, that preambular language does not set out binding obligations and merely provides support for a treaty interpreter.

As mentioned above, when a preamble refers to the objectives that emphasize the parties' intention to create "a stable framework for investments" or "favourable conditions for investments" as the sole aim of the treaty, this creates a possibility that tribunals will tend to resolve all interpretive uncertainties in favour of investors. In contrast, where a preamble complements investment promotion and protection objectives with other objectives such as sustainable development and the contracting States' right to regulate, this is likely to lead to more balanced interpretative outcomes.

For instance, in the preamble of their 2005 agreement, India and Singapore emphasize "their right to pursue economic philosophies suited to their development goals and their right to regulate activities to realize their national policy objectives". Some other treaty preambles have reaffirmed the contracting States' right to regulate,[2] mentioned other policy objectives such as sustainable development[3] as well as the States' commitment to human rights, labour and environmental standards.[4]

Comprehensive and well-worded treaty preambles can prove important in guiding the tribunal to the appropriate reading of the FET standard.

Option 6: Additional options to ensure the right to regulate

Option 4 states that an FET clause could include a clarification to the effect that the standard does not preclude States from adopting regulatory or other measures that pursue legitimate policy objectives. The preservation of the right to regulate is a concern not only in the context of the discussion on fair and equitable treatment; it is relevant for other IIA obligations, too. Therefore, it may be prudent to apply the right-to-regulate language to the treaty as a whole rather than to the FET standard alone. To this end, negotiators have a number of options at their disposal including the following:

(a) Reflecting the right to regulate as well as the general developmental purpose of an IIA in its preamble, which is often seen as reflecting the treaty's object and purpose and is therefore relevant for the interpretation of the treaty's individual provisions (see policy option 5 for details);

(b) Including in the treaty a "general exceptions" clause that affirms the host State's right to adopt measures necessary for, or related to, public policy objectives listed in the provision. Such clauses are often modelled on Article XX of the General Agreement on Tariffs and Trade (GATT) and Article XIV of the General Agreement on Trade in Services (GATS) and often include objectives such as the protection of human, animal or plant life or health, the conservation of exhaustible natural resources and the protection of public morals. The scope of exempted areas may vary from one treaty to another and should reflect policy priorities.

(c) The so-called "national security clauses" have an effect essentially similar to the "general exceptions" clauses; they traditionally exempt from the scope of the treaty's obligations State measures necessary for maintaining national security, public order, health and morality (UNCTAD, 2010b).

Some recent treaties include weak right-to-regulate clauses that should not be confused with the fully fledged exceptions. The EFTA -Ukraine FTA of 2010 offers an example:

*"Nothing in this Chapter shall be construed to prevent a Party from adopting, maintaining or enforcing any **measure consistent with this Chapter** that is in the public interest, such as measures to meet health, safety or environmental concerns or reasonable measures for prudential purposes"* [Article 4.8, emphasis added]

This provision may give an impression of exempting relevant health, safety, environmental or prudential measures from the treaty scope so that such measures cannot be held in violation of the treaty. However, this is not so – the words "consistent with this Chapter" suggest that the measures must still be in conformity with the treaty. If they are found not to be consistent with the obligations of the treaty, the State introducing such measures will be held liable for a breach. At most, this type of clause makes clear that the contracting parties have considered the possibility of a conflict between the treaty and the public-interest policies and that the latter may require special attention.

Important consideration: Preventing the nullification of the new FET language by virtue of the MFN clause

By attempting to rebalance the treaty obligations away from investor protection only, some of the policy options discussed above may be read as providing less favourable treatment to investors and their investments, compared with a country's other IIAs. If a State uses the new FET language in its new or renegotiated IIA or modifies its existing IIA, a claimant in ISDS proceedings may invoke the MFN clause of the new IIA in order to import a more favourable FET provision, for example, an unqualified FET obligation, from an earlier treaty.

To prevent this outcome, a State may wish to adapt the text of the MFN clause in the new treaty accordingly, i.e. exclude the possibility of importing substantive protections from earlier, and – if desired – even from subsequent, investment treaties (for model formulations, see UNCTAD, 2010a, pp. 107–109).[5]

* * *

Notes

[1] According to Article 38(1) of the ICJ Statute, applicable international legal sources include (a) international conventions establishing rules expressly recognized by the contesting States, (b) international custom, (c) the general principles of national law and (d) judicial decisions and the teachings of the most highly qualified publicists (as a subsidiary means for the determination of the rules of law).

[2] See, for example, the Panama-Taiwan FTA (2003).

[3] Canada-Colombia FTA (2008).

[4] Uruguay-United States BIT (2005); European Community-Cariforum Economic Partnership Agreement (2008).

[5] It should also be noted that at least two NAFTA tribunals have refused to allow claimants to import a purportedly more favourable FET clauses to replace the more restrictive FET text in NAFTA Article 1105. See *ADF v. United States*, Award, 2 October 2006, paras. 193–198; *Chemtura v. Canada*, Award, 2 August 2010, paras. 235–236.

REFERENCES

Abs H and Shawcross Lord Hartley (1960). The proposed convention to protect private foreign investment. *Journal of Public Law*. 9:115–124.

Brower II CH (2003). Structure, legitimacy and NAFTA's investment chapter. *Vanderbilt Journal of Transnational Law*. 36:37–94.

Brownlie I (2008). *Principles of Public International Law*. Seventh edition. Oxford University Press. Oxford.

Crawford J (1999). Second report on State responsibility to the International Law Commission, United Nations document A/CN.4/498. 17 March.

Dolzer R (2005). The impact of international investment treaties on domestic administrative law. *New York University Journal of International Law and Policy*. 37(4):953–972.

Dolzer R and Schreuer C (2008). *Principles of International Investment Law*. Oxford University Press. Oxford.

Douglas Z (2006). Nothing if not critical for investment treaty arbitration: *Occidental, Eureko* and *Methanex*. *Arbitration International*. 22:27–51.

Focarelli C (2009). Denial of justice. In: Wolfrum R, ed. *The Max Planck Encyclopedia of Public International Law*. Oxford University Press. Oxford. Available from www.mpepil.com .

Franck T (1995). *Fairness in International Law and Institutions* Clarendon Press. Oxford.

Gallus N (2005). The influence of the host State's level of development on international investment treaty standards of protection. *Journal of World Investment and Trade*. 6:711.

Jennings R and Watts A, eds. (1996). *Peace* (vol. I). *Oppenheim's International Law*. Ninth edition. Oxford University Press. Oxford.

Kinnear M (2008). The continuing development of the fair and equitable treatment standard. In: Andrea Bjorklund A et al., eds. *Investment Treaty Law: Current Issues III*. British Institute of International and Comparative Law:207–238. London.

Kläger R (2010). Fair and equitable treatment: A look at the theoretical underpinnings of legitimacy and fairness. *Journal of World Investment and Trade*. 11(3):435–455.

McLachlan C et al. (2007). *International Investment Arbitration: Substantive Principles*. Oxford University Press. Oxford.

Montt S (2009). *State Liability in Investment Treaty Arbitration*. Hart Publishing. Oxford and Portland.

Muchlinski P (2006). 'Caveat investor'? The relevance of the conduct of the investor under the fair and equitable treatment standard. *International and Comparative Law Quarterly*. 55:527–558.

Newcombe A and Paradell L (2009). *Law and Practice of Investment Treaties: Standards of Treatment*. Kluwer Law International.

Organisation for Economic Cooperation and Development (OECD) (1967). Council Resolution of 12 October 1967 on the Draft Convention on the Protection of Foreign Property. International Legal Materials. 7:117–143.

_____ (1984). Committee on International Investment and Multinational Enterprises. Intergovernmental agreements relating to investment in developing countries. Document No. 84/14. 27 May. OECD. Paris.

_____ (2004). Fair and equitable treatment standard in international investment law. *Working Papers on International Investment Law*. No. 2004/3. OECD. Paris. September.

The Oxford English Dictionary (1989). Second edition. Clarendon Press. Oxford.

Paparinskis M (2009). *International Minimum Standard and Fair and Equitable Treatment*. Doctoral thesis. Oxford University. Oxford. 28 September.

Paulsson J (2006). *Denial of Justice in International Law*. Cambridge University Press. Cambridge.

Porterfield M (2006). An international common law of investor rights? *University of Pennsylvania Journal of International Economic Law*.27:79–113.

Ripinsky S with Williams K (2008). *Damages in International Investment Law*. The British Institute of International and Comparative Law. London.

Roberts A (2010). Power and persuasion in investment treaty interpretation: The dual role of States. *American Journal of International Law*. 104:179–255.

Roth A (1949). *The Minimum Standard of Treatment in International Law*. Leiden.

Salacuse J (2010). *The Law of Investment Treaties*. Oxford University Press. Oxford.

Schemberg A (2008). Stabilization clauses and human rights. Report of 11 March 2008. Available from http://www.reports-and-materials.org/Stabilization-Clauses-and-Human-Rights-11-Mar-2008.pdf .

Schill S (2009). *The Multilateralization of International Investment Law.* Cambridge University Press. Cambridge.

_____ (2010). Fair and equitable treatment, the rule of law and comparative public law. In: Stephan Schill S, ed. *International Investment Law and Comparative Public Law.* Oxford University Press. Oxford.

Schreuer C (2005). Fair and equitable treatment in arbitral practice. *Journal of World Investment and Trade.* 5:357–386.

_____ (2007) Fair and equitable treatment: interactions with other standards. *Transnational Dispute Management.* 4(5).

Sornarajah M (2010). *The International Law on Foreign Investment.* Third edition. Cambridge University Press. Cambridge.

Thomas JC (2002). Reflections on article 1105 of NAFTA: History, state practice and the influence of commentators. *ICSID Review: Foreign Investment Law Journal.* 17(1):21–101.

UNCTAD (1999). *Fair and Equitable Treatment.* Series on Issues in International Investment Agreements. United Nations publication. Sales No.E.00.II.D.4. New York and Geneva.

_____ (2010a). *Most-Favoured-Nation Treatment: A Sequel.* United Nations publication. Sales No.E.00.II.D.19. New York and Geneva.

_____ (2010b). *The Protection of National Security in IIAs.* United Nations publication. Sales No. E.10.II.D.12. New York and Geneva.

_____ (2011). Interpretation of International Investment Agreements: What States Can Do. IIA Issue Note. Available from www.unctad.org/iia .

Vandevelde K (2010). A unified theory of fair and equitable treatment. *New York University Journal of International Law and Policy.* 43(1):43–106.

CASES AND ARBITRAL AWARDS

Unless indicated otherwise, the texts of arbitral awards and decisions can be found at http://italaw.com.

ADF Group Inc v. United States, ICSID Case No ARB(AF)/00/1 (NAFTA), Award, 9 January 2003.

Amto v. Ukraine, SCC Case No. 080/2005 (Energy Charter Treaty), Final Award, 26 March 2008.

Azinian, Davitian, & Baca v. Mexico, ICSID Case No. ARB(AF)/97/2 (NAFTA), Award, 1 November 1999, 14 ICSID Rev-FILJ 538 (1999).

Azurix v. Argentina, ICSID Case No. ARB/01/12 (Argentina-United States BIT), Award, 14 July 2006.

Bayindir Insaat Turizm Ticaret ve Sanayi A Ş v. Pakistan, ICSID Case No ARB/03/29 (Pakistan-Turkey BIT), Award, 27 August 2009.

Biwater Gauff (Tanzania) Ltd v. Tanzania, ICSID Case No ARB/05/22 (Tanzania-UK BIT), Award and Concurring and Dissenting Opinion, 24 July 2008.

Cargill v. Mexico, ICSID Case No. ARB(AF)/05/2 (NAFTA), Award, 18 September 2009.

Chemtura Corporation v. Canada, UNCITRAL Rules (NAFTA), Award, 2 August 2010.

CMS Gas Transmission Company v. Argentina, ICSID Case No. ARB/01/8 (Argentina-United States BIT), Award, 12 May 2005, 44 ILM 1205 (2005).

Compañía de Aguas del Aconquija s.a. and Vivendi Universal S.A. v. Argentina, ICSID Case No. ARB/97/3 (Argentina-France BIT), Award, 20 August 2007.

Continental Casualty Company v. Argentina, ICSID Case No.ARB/03/9 (Argentina-United States BIT), Award, 5 September 2008.

Desert Line Projects LLC v. Yemen, ICSID Case No. ARB/05/17, (Oman-Yemen BIT), Award, 6 February 2008.

Duke Energy Electroquil Partners and Electroquil SA v. Ecuador, ICSID Case No ARB/04/19 (Ecuador-US BIT), Award, 18 August 2008.

EDF International S.A., SAUR International S.A. and León Participaciones Argentinas S.A. v. Romania, ICSID Case No. ARB/05/13 (Argentina-Belgium and Luxembourg Economic Union BIT and Argentina-France BIT), Award, 8 October 2009.

Enron Corporation and Ponderosa Assets, L.P. v. Argentina, ICSID Case No. ARB/01/3 (Argentina-United States BIT), Award, 22 May 2007.

FTR Holding S.A. (Switzerland), Philip Morris Products S.A. (Switzerland) and Abal Hermanos S.A. (Uruguay) v. Oriental Republic of Uruguay, ICSID Case No. ARB/10/7 (Switzerland-Uruguay BIT), registered 26 March 2010.

GAMI Investments, Inc. v. Mexico, UNCITRAL Rules (NAFTA), Final Award, 15 November 2004.

Genin and others v. Estonia, ICSID Case No. ARB/99/2 (Estonia-United States BIT), Award, 25 June 2001, ICSID Rev-FILJ395 (2002).

Glamis Gold v. United States, UNCITRAL Rules (NAFTA), Award, 8 June 2009.

Grand River Enterprises Six Nations, Ltd., et al. v. United States of America, UNICTRAL Rules (NAFTA), Award, 12 January 2011.

Gustav F W Hamester GmbH & Co KG v. Republic of Ghana, ICSID Case No. ARB/07/24 (Germany-Ghana BIT), Award, 18 June 2010.

Helnan International Hotels A/S v. Egypt, ICSID Case No. ARB/05/09 (Denmark-Egypt), Award, 3 July 2008.

International Thunderbird Gaming Corporation v. Mexico, UNCITRAL Rules (NAFTA), Award, 26 January 2006.

Jan de Nul N.V. and Dredging International N.V. v. Arab Republic of Egypt, ICSID Case No. ARB/04/13 (Belgium-Luxembourg-Egypt BIT), Award, 6 November 2008.

Ioannis Kardassopoulos and Ron Fuchs v. The Republic of Georgia, ICSID Case Nos. ARB/05/18 and ARB/07/15 (Georgia-Greece BIT and the Energy Charter Treaty), Award, 10 March 2010.

LG&E v. Argentina, ICSID Case No. ARB/02/1 (Argentina-United States BIT), Decision on Liability, 3 October 2006.

Loewen Group, Inc. and Raymond L. Loewen v. United States, ICSID Case No. ARB (AF)/98/3 (NAFTA), Award, 26 June 2003, 42 ILM 811 (2003).

Maffezini v. Spain, ICSID Case No. ARB/97/7 (Argentina-Spain BIT), Award, 13 November 2000, 16 ICSID Rev-FILJ 248 (2001).

M.C.I. Power Group L.C. and New Turbine, Inc. v. Ecuador, ICSID Case No. ARB/03/6 (Ecuador-United States BIT), Award, 31 July 2007.

Merrill & Ring Forestry L.P. v. Canada, UNCITRAL Rules (NAFTA), Award, 31 March 2010.

Metalclad Corporation v. Mexico, ICSID Case No ARB (AF)/97/1 (NAFTA), Award, 30 August 2000, 40 ILM 36 (2001).

Metalpar S.A. and Buen Aire S.A. v. Argentine Republic, ICSID Case No. ARB/03/5 (Argentina-Chile BIT), Award, 6 June 2008.

Methanex v. United States, UNCITRAL (NAFTA) Final Award on Jurisdiction and Merits, 3 August 2005:

Mondev International Ltd v: United States; ICSID Case No. ARB (AF)/99/2 (NAFTA), Award; 11 October 2002.

MTD Equity Sdn. Bhd. & MTD Chile S.A. v. Chile, ICSID Case No. ARB/01/7 (Chile-Malaysia BIT), Award, 25 May 2004, 44 ILM 91 (2005).

S.D. Myers Inc. v. Canada, UNCITRAL Rules (NAFTA), First Partial Award, 13 November 2000, 40 ILM 1408 (2001).

LFH Neer and Pauline Neer (United States v. Mexico) (1926) 4 RIAA 60.

Noble Ventures v. Romania, ICSID Case No.ARB/01/11 (Romania-United States BIT), Award, 12 October 2005.

Occidental Exploration and Production Co v. Ecuador, UNCITRAL rules, Administered Case No. UN 3467 (Ecuador-United States BIT), Award, 1 July 2004.

Parkerings-Compagniet AS v. Lithuania, ICSID Case No. ARB/05/8 (Lithuania-Norway BIT), Award, 11 September 2007.

Plama Consortium Limited v. Bulgaria, ICSID Case No. ARB/03/24 (Energy Charter Treaty), Award, 27 August 2008.

Pope and Talbot v. Canada, UNCITRAL rules (NAFTA), Award on the Merits of Phase 2, 10 April 2001.

Pope and Talbot v. Canada, UNCITRAL rules (NAFTA), Award in Respect of Damages, 31 May 2002, 41 ILM 1347 (2002).

PSEG Global, Inc., The North American Coal Corporation, and Konya Ingin Electrik Uretim ve Ticaret Limited Sirketi v. Republic of Turkey, ICSID Case No. ARB/02/5 (Turkey-United States BIT), Award, 19 January 2007.

Rumeli Telekom AS and Telsim Mobil Telekomikasyon Hizmetleri AS v. Kazakhstan, ICSID Case No ARB/05/16 (Kazakhstan- Turkey BIT), Award, 29 July 2008.

Saluka Investments BV (The Netherlands) v. Czech Republic. UNCITRAL Rules (Czech Republic-Netherlands BIT), Partial Award, 17 March 2006.

Sempra Energy International v. Argentina, ICSID Case No.ARB/02/16 (Argentina-United States BIT), Award, 28 September 2007.

Siemens AG v. Argentina, ICSID Case No ARB/02/8 (Argentina-Germany BIT), Award on Jurisdiction, 3 August 2004, 44 ILM 138 (2005).

Técnicas Medioambientales Tecmed, S.A. v. Mexico, ICSID Case No ARB (AF)/00/2 (Mexico-Spain BIT), Award, 29 May 2003, 43 ILM 133 (2004).

United Parcel Service of America Inc. v. Canada, UNCITRAL Rules (NAFTA), Award on Jurisdiction, 22 November 2002.

Waste Management v. Mexico, ICSID Case No ARB(AF)/00/3 (NAFTA), Award, 30 April 2004, 43 ILM 967 (2004).

International Court of Justice

Barcelona Traction Light and Power Company Limited (Belgium v. Spain), Judgment, *I.C.J. Reports* 1970, p. 3.

Tunisia-Libya Continental Shelf Case, I.C.J. Reports 1982, p. 18.

Case Concerning Elettronica Sicula S.p.A (ELSI) (United States v. Italy), I.C.J. Reports 1989, p. 15.

Case Concerning Ahmadou Sadio Diallo (Guinea v. Democratic Republic of the Congo), Preliminary Objections, General List No.103 Judgment 24 May 2007. Available from http://www.icj-cij.org/docket/files/103/13856.pdf.

British Columbia, Canada

United Mexican States v. Metalclad Corp., 2001, BCSC 664, 2 March 2001, Tysoe J.

SELECTED UNCTAD PUBLICATIONS ON INTERNATIONAL INVESTMENT AGREEMENTS, TRANSNATIONAL CORPORATIONS AND FOREIGN DIRECT INVESTMENT

(For more information, please visit www.unctad.org/en/pub .)

World Investment Reports
(For more information, visit www.unctad.org/wir .)

World Investment Report 2011. Non-Equity Modes of International Production and Development. Sales No. E.11.II.D.2. $95. Available from http://www.unctad.org/en/docs//wir2011_en.pdf.

World Investment Report 2010. Investing in a Low-Carbon Economy. Sales No. E.10.II.D.1. $80. Available from http://www.unctad.org/en/docs//wir2010_en.pdf.

World Investment Report 2009. Transnational Corporations, Agricultural Production and Development. Sales No. E.09.II.D.15. $80. Available from http://www.unctad.org/en/docs/wir2009_en.pdf.

World Investment Report 2008. Transnational Corporations and the Infrastructure Challenge. Sales No. E.08.II.D.23. $80. Available from http://www.unctad.org/en/docs//wir2008_en.pdf.

World Investment Report 2007. Transnational Corporations, Extractive Industries and Development. Sales No. E.07.II.D.9. $75. Available from http://www.unctad.org/ en/docs//wir2007_en.pdf.

World Investment Report 2006. FDI from Developing and Transition Economies: Implications for Development. Sales No. E.06.II.D.11. $75. Available from http://www.unctad.org/ en/docs//wir2006_en.pdf.

World Investment Report 2005. Transnational Corporations and the Internationalization of R&D. Sales No. E.05.II.D.10. $75. Available from http://www.unctad.org/ en/docs//wir2005_en.pdf.

World Investment Report 2004. The Shift Towards Services. Sales No. E.04.II.D.36. $75. Available from http://www.unctad.org/en/docs//wir2004_en.pdf.

World Investment Report 2003. FDI Policies for Development: National and International Perspectives. Sales No. E.03.II.D.8. $49. Available from http://www.unctad.org/ en/docs//wir2003_en.pdf.

World Investment Report 2002: Transnational Corporations and Export Competitiveness. 352 p. Sales No. E.02.II.D.4. $49. Available from http://www.unctad.org/ en/docs//wir2002_en.pdf.

World Investment Report 2001: Promoting Linkages. 356 p. Sales No. E.01.II.D.12 $49. Available from http://www.unctad.org/wir/contents/wir01content.en.htm.

World Investment Report 2000: Cross-border Mergers and Acquisitions and Development. 368 p. Sales No. E.99.II.D.20. $49. Available from http://www.unctad.org/wir/ contents/wir00content.en.htm.

Ten Years of World Investment Reports: The Challenges Ahead. Proceedings of an UNCTAD special event on future challenges in the area of FDI. UNCTAD/ITE/Misc.45. Available from http://www.unctad.org/wir.

International Investment Policies for Development
(For more information, visit http://www.unctad.org/iia .)

Investor-State Disputes: Prevention and Alternatives to Arbitration. 129 p. Sales no. E.10.II.D.11. $20.

Investor–State Disputes: Prevention and Alternatives to Arbitration II. 214 p. Available from http://www.unctad.org/en/docs/webdiaeia20108_en.pdf

The Role of International Investment Agreements in Attracting Foreign Direct Investment to Developing Countries. 161 p. Sales no. E.09.II.D.20. $22.

The Protection of National Security in IIAs. 170 p. Sales no. E.09.II.D.12. $15.

Identifying Core Elements in Investment Agreements in the APEC Regions. 134 p. Sales no. E.08.II.D.27. $15.

International Investment Rule-Making: Stocktaking, Challenges and the Way Forward. 124 p. Sales no. E.08.II.D.1. $15.

Investment Promotion Provisions in International Investment Agreements. 103 p. Sales no. E.08.II.D.5. $15.

Investor-State Dispute Settlement and Impact on Investment Rulemaking. 110 p. Sales No. E.07.II.D.10. $30.

Bilateral Investment Treaties 1995–2006: Trends in Investment Rulemaking. 172 p. Sales No. E.06.II.D.16. $30.

Investment Provisions in Economic Integration Agreements. 174 p. UNCTAD/ITE/IIT/2005/10.

Preserving Flexibility in IIAs: The Use of Reservations. 104 p. Sales no.: E.06.II.D.14. $15.

International Investment Arrangements: Trends and Emerging Issues. 110 p. Sales No. E.06.II.D.03. $15.

Investor-State Disputes Arising from Investment Treaties: A Review. 106 p. Sales No. E.06.II.D.1 $15

South–South Cooperation in Investment Arrangements. 108 p. Sales No. E.05.II.D.26 $15.

International Investment Agreements in Services. 119 p. Sales No. E.05.II.D.15. $15.

The REIO Exception in MFN Treatment Clauses. 92 p. Sales No. E.05.II.D.1. $15.

Issues in International Investment Agreements
(For more information, visit http://www.unctad.org/iia .)

Scope and Definition: A Sequel. 149 p. Sales No. E.11.II.D.9. $25.

Most-Favoured-Nation Treatment: A Sequel. 141 p. Sales No. E.10.II.D.19. $25.

International Investment Agreements: Key Issues, Volumes I, II and *III.* Sales No.: E.05.II.D.6. $65.

State Contracts. 84 p. Sales No. E.05.II.D.5. $15.

Competition. 112 p. E.04.II.D.44. $ 15.

Key Terms and Concepts in IIAs: a Glossary. 232 p. Sales No. E.04.II.D.31. $15.

Incentives. 108 p. Sales No. E.04.II.D.6. $15.

Transparency. 118 p. Sales No. E.04.II.D.7. $15.

Dispute Settlement: State-State. 101 p. Sales No. E.03.II.D.6. $15.

Dispute Settlement: Investor-State. 125 p. Sales No. E.03.II.D.5. $15.

Transfer of Technology. 138 p. Sales No. E.01.II.D.33. $18.

Illicit Payments. 108 p. Sales No. E.01.II.D.20. $13.

Home Country Measures. 96 p. Sales No.E.01.II.D.19. $12.

Host Country Operational Measures. 109 p. Sales No E.01.II.D.18. $15.

Social Responsibility. 91 p. Sales No. E.01.II.D.4. $15.

Environment. 105 p. Sales No. E.01.II.D.3. $15.

Transfer of Funds. 68 p. Sales No. E.00.II.D.27. $12.

Flexibility for Development. 185 p. Sales No. E.00.II.D.6. $15.

Employment. 69 p. Sales No. E.00.II.D.15. $12.

Taxation. 111 p. Sales No. E.00.II.D.5. $12.

Taking of Property. 83 p. Sales No. E.00.II.D.4. $12.

National Treatment. 94 p. Sales No. E.99.II.D.16. $12.

Admission and Establishment. 69 p. Sales No. E.99.II.D.10. $12.

Trends in International Investment Agreements: An Overview. 133 p. Sales No. E.99.II.D.23. $12.

Lessons from the MAI. 52 p. Sales No. E.99.II.D.26. $10.

Fair and Equitable Treatment. 85 p. Sales No. E.99.II.D.15. $12.

Transfer Pricing. 71 p. Sales No. E.99.II.D.8. $12.

Scope and Definition. 93 p. Sales No. E.99.II.D.9. $12.

Most-Favoured Nation Treatment. 57 p. Sales No. E.99.II.D.11. $12.

Investment-Related Trade Measures. 57 p. Sales No. E.99.II.D.12. $12.

Foreign Direct Investment and Development. 74 p. Sales No. E.98.II.D.15. $12.

Investment Policy Monitors

Investment Policy Monitor. A periodic report by the UNCTAD secretariat. No. 3, 7 October 2010. Available from http://www.unctad.org/en/docs/webdiaeia20105_en.pdf .

Investment Policy Monitor. A periodic report by the UNCTAD secretariat. No. 2, 20 April 2010. Available from http://www.unctad.org/en/docs/webdiaeia20102_en.pdf .

Investment Policy Monitor. A periodic report by the UNCTAD secretariat. No. 1, 4 December 2009. Available from http://www.unctad.org/en/docs/webdiaeia200911_en.pdf .

IIA Monitors and Issues Notes

IIA Issues Note No. 1 (2010): Latest Developments in Investor–State Dispute Settlement.
Available from http://www.unctad.org/en/docs/webdiaeia20103_en.pdf .

IIA Monitor No. 3 (2009): Recent developments in international investment agreements (2008–June 2009).
Available from http://www.unctad.org/en/docs/webdiaeia20098_en.pdf .

IIA Monitor No. 2 (2009): Selected Recent Developments in IIA Arbitration and Human Rights.
Available from http://www.unctad.org/en/docs/webdiaeia20097_en.pdf .

IIA Monitor No. 1 (2009): Latest Developments in Investor–State Dispute Settlement.
Available from http://www.unctad.org/en/docs/webdiaeia20096_en.pdf .

IIA Monitor No. 2 (2008): Recent developments in international investment agreements (2007–June 2008).
http://www.unctad.org/en/docs/webdiaeia20081_en.pdf .

IIA Monitor No. 1 (2008): Latest Developments in Investor– State Dispute Settlement.
Available from http://www.unctad.org/en/docs/iteiia20083_en.pdf .

IIA Monitor No. 3 (2007): Recent developments in international investment agreements (2006–June 2007).
Available from http://www.unctad.org/en/docs/webiteiia20076_en.pdf .

IIA Monitor No. 2 (2007): Development implications of international investment agreements.
Available from http://www.unctad.org/en/docs/webiteiia20072_en.pdf .

IIA Monitor No. 1 (2007): Intellectual Property Provisions in International Investment Arrangements.
Available from http://www.unctad.org/en/docs/webiteiia20071_en.pdf .

IIA Monitor No. 4 (2006): Latest Developments in Investor-State Dispute Settlement.
Available from http://www.unctad.org/sections/dite_pcbb/docs/webiteiia200611_en.pdf .

IIA Monitor No. 3 (2006): The Entry into Force of Bilateral Investment Treaties (BITs).
Available from http://www.unctad.org/en/docs/webiteiia20069_en.pdf .

IIA Monitor No. 2 (2006): Developments in international investment agreements in 2005.
Available from http://www.unctad.org/en/docs/webiteiia20067_en.pdf .

IIA Monitor No. 1 (2006): Systemic Issues in International Investment Agreements (IIAs).
Available from http://www.unctad.org/en/docs/webiteiia20062_en.pdf .

IIA Monitor No. 4 (2005): Latest Developments in Investor-State Dispute Settlement.
Available from http://www.unctad.org/en/docs/webiteiit20052_en.pdf .

IIA Monitor No. 2 (2005): Recent Developments in International Investment Agreements.
Available from http://www.unctad.org/en/docs/webiteiit20051_en.pdf .

IIA Monitor No. 1 (2005): South–South Investment Agreements Proliferating.
Available from http://www.unctad.org/en/docs/webiteiit20061_en.pdf .

United Nations publications may be obtained from bookstores and distributors throughout the world. Please consult your bookstore or write to the addresses listed below.

For Africa, Asia and Europe:

Sales Section
United Nations Office at Geneva
Palais des Nations
CH-1211 Geneva 10
Switzerland
Telephone: (41-22) 917-1234
Fax: (41-22) 917-0123
E-mail: unpubli@unog.ch

For Asia and the Pacific, the Caribbean, Latin America and North America:

Sales Section
Room DC2-0853
United Nations Secretariat
New York, NY 10017
United States
Telephone: (1-212) 963-8302 or (800) 253-9646
Fax: (1-212) 963-3489
E-mail: publications@un.org

All prices are quoted in United States dollars.

For further information on the work of the Division on Investment and Enterprise, UNCTAD, please address inquiries to:

United Nations Conference on Trade and Development
Division on Investment and Enterprise
Palais des Nations, Room E-10054
CH-1211 Geneva 10, Switzerland
Telephone: (41-22) 917-5651
Telefax: (41-22) 917-0498
http://www.unctad.org

QUESTIONNAIRE

Fair and Equitable Treatment: A Sequel
Sales No. E.10.II.D.15

In order to improve the quality and relevance of the work of the UNCTAD Division on Investment, Technology and Enterprise Development, it would be useful to receive the views of readers on this publication. It would therefore be greatly appreciated if you could complete the following questionnaire and return it to:

Readership Survey
UNCTAD Division on Investment and Enterprise
United Nations Office at Geneva
Palais des Nations, Room E-9123
CH-1211 Geneva 10, Switzerland
Fax: 41-22-917-0194

1. Name and address of respondent (optional):

    _____

    _____

2. Which of the following best describes your area of work?

Government	☐	Public enterprise	☐
Private enterprise	☐	Academic or research institution	☐
International organization	☐	Media	☐
Not-for-profit organization	☐	Other (specify) _____	

3. In which country do you work? _____

4. What is your assessment of the contents of this publication?

| Excellent | ☐ | Adequate | ☐ |
| Good | ☐ | Poor | ☐ |

5. How useful is this publication to your work?

| Very useful | ☐ | Somewhat useful | ☐ |
| Irrelevant | ☐ | | |

6. Please indicate the three things you liked best about this publication:

_____

_____

_____

7. Please indicate the three things you liked least about this publication:

_____

_____

_____

8. If you have read other publications of the UNCTAD Division on Investment, Enterprise Development and Technology, what is your overall assessment of them?

| Consistently good | ☐ | Usually good, but with some exceptions | ☐ |
| Generally mediocre | ☐ | Poor | ☐ |

9. On average, how useful are those publications to you in your work?

    Very useful   ☐   Somewhat useful   ☐
    Irrelevant   ☐

10. Are you a regular recipient of *Transnational Corporations* (formerly *The CTC Reporter*), UNCTAD-DITE's tri-annual refereed journal?

    Yes ☐   No ☐

    If not, please check here if you would like to receive a sample copy sent to the name and address you have given above: ☐